THE
NAIJA FOOD
PHILOSOPHER

BY

DR WILSON ORHIUNU
(Babawilly)

The Naija Food Philosopher
Copyright © 2020 by Dr. Wilson Orhiunu

Published by
Dr. Wilson Orhiunu
Email: babawill2000@gmail.com

ISBN 978-0-9551390-2-4

Book cover Photograph by Kemi Akiyode-Adebayo

taken at Pitanga Restaurant. London

Book Cover Concept: Serena Adeyanju

Book Cover Design: Optimist_Designs

Printed in the United Kingdom

Contents

$\mathscr{D}$edication

THIS BOOK IS DEDICATED TO MY MOTHER, Mrs Charity Orhiunu (Nee Onokhurefe), a woman who has always carried herself with dignity no matter what the situation was.

She provided nourishment for me when I was most vulnerable, and for that, I am eternally grateful.

Acknowledgements

IN WRITING THE NAIJA FOOD PHILOSOPHER, I have drawn on personal experiences that I have shared with so many people. Most of my dining table time is with friends and family, so this book is essentially about them.

In September 2017, I ran a series of posts on my Facebook page under the title: Naija Food month, and I chose The Naija Food Philosopher as a name to go with the series. There was a different article most days, and come October 2017, I had quite a lot of materials. They were articles and poems themed around Nigerian food.

I have received numerous comments and encouragements from many people—too numerous to name. I would like to thank Titilayo Orhiunu for editing some of the early articles which were posted on the internet Journal QED.NG whose editor, Olumide Iyanda, has also been gracious and kind to me.

I would also like to thank my long-term friend from the University of Benin who have helped me with various aspects of the manuscript and have encouraged me to write. Reverend Divine Ayela and Dr Anne Nwebube, you both have been great. Angela Onelum, you were very gracious when you told me that I had talent in the 90s. God bless you.

Furthermore, I would like to thank my children for spurring me to write without even saying a word, the same way I spur them at the dinner table with the admonition: "Finish your food."

Finally, in God we trust.

PARTY JOLLOF RICE

A party without jollof rice,
is that one too a party?

A FEAST IS MADE FOR MERRY, AND FOR THE vast majority of West Africans, there is only so far that nice music and drinks can go. At some point, guests want to be asked the question that is like Mozart to their ears: "white, fried or jollof?"

The answer is usually, "Jollof, please."

Some need moin-moin to eat their jollof rice and would opt for fried or white rice in its absence. Others need dodo (fried plantain) with their jollof rice and might get by with a banana if the dodo has run out.

A party where the dodo did not run out,
is that one too a party?

One must mention the rare breed of Nigerians — the ones with rice allergies which can be distressing. After three spoons of jollof rice, they develop streaming eyes and noses which

11

would make people inquire if "the pepper is too much."

A full-blown asthma attack may develop and paranoid family members may start to accuse each other of intentional poisoning. It is a sad thing to be told by your doctor the unpalatable news: no more rice! The distraught patient asks how they would celebrate weddings, birthdays, and meaningless (party-for-party-sake) gatherings if they cannot eat rice.

A Nigerian that cannot eat party jollof rice,
is that one also a Nigerian?

The ability to consume rice is almost a legal requirement in Nigeria. The average Nigerian eats about 24.8kg of rice annually. As would be expected, some will love eating rice more than others. For some, it is an act of worship. They dream of rice all night and eat it all day.

Everyone is free to determine their nutritional destiny, but one must always make provision for whatever appetites one decides to generate.

Take the Kenyans, for instance, who are the highest tea drinkers in Africa and number four in the world. They are also the world's third-largest producers of tea, so there is a balance.

The UK grows no tea but rank number twelve among the world tea drinkers' league. Through brands like Lipton tea and Tetley Tea, UK businesses make a profit from the tea business and actually do better for themselves than the tea farmers. No matter what you learnt in school, once you live in the UK, you slowly start to forget that cocoa, tea, and coffee are not grown there because the really strong brands for these products are based in Europe.

The story is different in Nigeria where about seven million metric tonnes of rice is consumed annually with local production of 2.7 million metric tonnes. The shortfall is imported and costs the country about one billion naira a day. In just one month, the proverbial 30 billion leaves the *account.*

China and India love their rice and eat more of it than Nigerians but there are differences. Firstly, these countries know not the pleasures of party jollof rice and secondly, they grow what they eat and sell the rest to other countries, creating a lot of local jobs in the process.

Nigeria is very good with cassava. We make a lot of it, and it is used to produce the staple food, garri. Yam production is not bad and could be increased. I wonder if Nigerians could go for a whole year without rice.

There are people who have been without electricity for one year, and they seem to be coping. But take away their rice, and they might become suicide bombers! The cost of rice keeps going up and people keep on buying it. Soon, things might fall apart because there is a limit to how much the average man can pay for a plate of rice.

Personally, I don't trust rice too much. Is it not one of those plants that take up the arsenic in the surrounding soil? It is the government's job to ensure that the arsenic content of rice does not exceed safe levels. Who wants poison in their party jollof rice?

And then, there are all these rumours about fake foods everywhere on the internet.

Finally, rice is a carbohydrate, and that means it is converted to sugar in the body. Most people over forty years of age have no business eating more than six tablespoons of rice at a sitting, yet many eat it by the pot-loads.

It might help to develop alternative recipes like party jollof eba or party jollof yam pottage. Other foodstuffs need to be glamorised and promoted until the local production of rice in Nigeria can meet and perhaps exceed the demand.

Hope springs eternal. I have a dream that one

day, in a thousand parties in Nigeria on a Saturday night, the plates of party jollof rice would all be alumni of our local farms, standing side by side with moin-moin and plantain that have been locally sourced. I have a dream that the beef on all Nigerian plates would be conflict-free.

Rice will grow abundantly in the land of Nigeria as it does worldwide. Yes, rice is akin to a bronze medallist in the planting and cultivation Olympic Finals. Sugar cane and maize take gold and silver respectively. Rice is the third most planted crop on Earth.

What grows in China and India can grow in Nigeria. No shaking.

A country that cannot feed its population,
is that one too a country?

PS: Jollof rice was invented by aliens on Mars and sent down to Senegal, Ghana, and Nigeria at 2 pm on the second day of March 419 AD. It floated down in a bright giant space pot. The aliens then went on to supply Wakanda with Vibranium.

The rest, as they say, is history, lies, and deception.

References

1. An Overview of the Nigerian Rice Economy by Prof Tunji Akande Economic Analysis of Rice Consumption Patterns in Nigeria

2. S. B. Fakayode 1, O. A. Omotesho1, and A. E. Omoniwa1 J. Agr. Sci. Tech. (2010) Vol. 12: 135-144

She No Sabi Cook

Babawilly tak say…
We all have our talents
Rare gifts, peculiar traits
And judging from her many kids,
She has talented ovaries
Yet come the kitchen-matics
Her sums just don't add up
She started off baking a cake
And ended up with hard bread
That babe no sabi cook
It's true just cannot cook
Town crier warn the neighbourhood
That lady just can't cook

I found out just last Christmas
When invited out for lunch
While everyone was saying grace
I opened up my eyes
I saw the little fish
Kissing the giant shrimp

The fish said to his lover:
"We will continue in his stomach."
That babe no sabi cook
It's true just cannot cook
Town crier warn the neighbourhood
That lady just can't cook

I didn't learn my lesson
Went there for Easter lunch
She served one kain egusi soup
That looked like an oil spill
Palm oil floats above
Submerged vegetables
Was on the loo all night,
And in the morning saw my doctor
That babe no sabi cook
It's true just cannot cook
Town crier warn the neighbourhood
That lady just can't cook

I am here to watch football
Upon their giant screen
He has told her to cook something.
We will eat in half time."
She brought a mountain in

I said, "Thanks for the Tuwo."
She snapped, "Don't mention Mr Neighbour,
But it's actually jollof rice."
That babe no sabi cook
It's true just cannot cook
Town crier warn the neighbourhood
That lady just can't cook.

The return match was at nine
My babe cooked for half time
Smooth pounded yam, ogbono soup
With fish and chicken thighs
My neighbour licked his plate clean
Then begged for a second round
I told him food has finished, and he
Should eat when he gets home
That babe no sabi cook
It's true just cannot cook
Town crier warn the neighbourhood
That lady just can't cook

He looked at me with bad eye
As if it was my fault
He fell in love with Miss Alchemist
Parading as a chef.

His phone went off so sudden
His dinner was now served
He walked with Africa on his head
As he moved towards his poison
That babe no sabi cook
It's true just cannot cook
Town crier warn the neighbourhood
That lady just can't cook.

Ukodo Tonight

1   *It's Ukodo Tonight*
   Finger licking, licking good
   We are doing alright.
   You're my woman.
   I'm your man.

2   *Been at work*
   Since 9 o'clock
   But it's now five.
   Hey!
   That boss of mine
   Works me to the bone,
   But it's now five.
   Ahh!

3   *Tonight's the night*
   We celebrate our love
   You've been to Igbudu market
   To buy choice yams,
   Some crayfish
   Alligator pepper
   And dry fish.

I am on my way home
For Ukodo tonight

4   *It's been twelve months*
Since we said "I do"
Oh, how sweet time flies.
With a candlelit dinner,
We are insured against NEPA.
Let's celebrate.
We have made it this far.
Stir that boiling froth real slow.
Yes, my appetite is higher
Than any Warri TV aerial
For Ukodo tonight

5   *I am driving through*
The streets of Warri reminiscing
About how it was at the start.
For Mama said
It wouldn't work.
Papa said
It wouldn't last,
Brother said
It wouldn't work
Sister said
It wouldn't last.
But here we are getting ready
For Ukodo tonight.

6   *The smell fills the compound.*
Neighbours know what you are cooking.
So pull out the phone
And lock the doors.
Shut the windows
And draw the curtains.
Even if the President comes knocking
We no dey house.
For it's Ukodo tonight.

7   *This love grows*
Stronger every day.
So fan the flames
of a love
that just wouldn't die.
Soft music plays
As you turn the palm oil,
on hot yams so soft
and tender,
I'll rather be nowhere else
Than here
For Ukodo tonight

Kola Nut Love

She is blessed
By the ancestors
Two big Kola Nuts
On her chest
They speak to me:
"We bring Kola;
We bring life."
She cuts away my sadness
With a tongue like a knife

Two gifts so smooth that move
With each dainty step towards me
She sits on two sacred Kola Nuts
Soft cushions for my hands
This Kola keeps me alert
Chased the sleep like a masquerade
I nibble when it is full moon
I savour the taste in the light breeze
She brought Kola, She brought life

UKODO FOR MY LOVE

EMERHO HAD ALWAYS KNOWN HOW TO MAKE an entrance. With his impeccable timing and canny instinct for the dramatic, he strode into the crowded market and caused immediate pandemonium. Not since Chief Okpako's two wives had fought fiercely in this same market, tearing the clothes off each other, had a crowd gathered so fast.

There were gasps of wonder as Emerho walked with strong and decisive steps towards Onoriode's stall in the market.

This was the great market day in the town of Ogheli. The harvest was over, and there was nothing to do while waiting for the next planting season. Nothing to do except go to the market or go fishing. It was on the river that fortune and fate conspired to smile on Emerho for he had caught the biggest catfish seen in living memory. Six other fishermen had gone over to help him with his battle to lift the fish into his sinking canoe.

All activities stopped at the river. Everyone followed the catfish. Maidens left water pots, and fishermen abandoned their canoes, all wanted to see the reaction on the faces of people when they saw the fish. Some of the glory would naturally go to the eyewitnesses as they told of what they had seen. Four men had carried the fish, but as soon as they approached the main part of the market, Emerho had insisted that he would carry the huge catch on his back even if the weight killed him.

Onoriode was paralysed with a thousand emotions when she saw Emerho drop his load in front of her stall on top of a makeshift tray of banana leaves that had been hastily gathered. His torso glistened with sweat. Then he did it. He contracted his breast muscles in quick succession. It was a trick he had learnt and perfected years ago. The effect on Onoriode was the same. She became oblivious to the cheering crowd and looked him deep in the eyes. Emerho understood the language of her eyes. She looked at him that way last night before she said what she always said when she was in the mood for love.

"If I handle you, Emerho, you will see your mother and call her your sister."

Onoriode bit her lower lip and wiped the sweat off her brow. Emerho twitched his chest muscles again; he loved to tease her.

Onoriode always said she married him for his muscles. It reminded her of the village of Oropke which had fenced compounds. Onoriode always said she knew where each of Emerho's muscles started and ended, as the boundaries were very visible. Unlike Ochuko, the suitor her father had wanted for her. At the time, she had said to Ochuko that his body reminded her of their village; a lot of houses and compounds built closely together. No one knew where one compound ended and another started.

Chief Okpako was soon at the scene. He was the Ovie of Ogheli and rarely ventured outside his royal palace to the market. Today, however, was different. His wives had rushed into his room screaming, "You have to see it!"

His royal highness prayed to Oghene, the great creator and thanked him for the fish, which was obviously a sign of many blessings to come. After all, had Ogheli not just come out of the most successful yam harvest ever seen anywhere in the world? He also thanked his ancestors for giving his son, Emerho, the strong spine to pull out such a leviathan from the depths. "May the ancestors strengthen the other parts that have not been strengthened in you" was how he ended his prayers, hinting at Emerho's childless marriage. A resounding ise rent the air.

His royal highness was not partial to a bit of greed as whispered to one of his wives who in turn whispered to Onoriode.

Onoriode walked over to Emerho and hugged him. "The shameless goat says he would have the tail end of the fish," she said in his ear making him laugh out noisily. It was a day of celebration, and Emerho didn't mind sharing his good fortune. He signalled for a machete to be brought to him and in eight sharp strokes, he had the fish split into two, drawing gasps from the crowd.

The young men of the town suddenly broke out into a song and lifted their new hero shoulder-high, singing and running in the direction of his house.

Emerho has wrestled a great fish and won

Emerho has wrestled his great farm and won

Emerho has wrestled his beautiful wife and won

There is nothing our champion cannot do.

Onoriode beamed with pride as she gave instructions to her friend to mind her stall for her. As soon as she saw the fish, she knew that tonight was the night she was destined to cook Emerho a meal he had never eaten before, a recipe revealed to her in a dream by her late mother. "Emerho will lick his fingers tonight," she said under her breath, smiling mischievously to herself.

As Onoriode walked home, she remembered her mother as she always appeared in her dreams. She wore a spotless white scarf on her head and tied a white wrapper across her chest. She spoke with the most soothing of voices that calmed all Onoriode's fears in a way only a mother could. Onoriode was eight years old when her mother died. She first appeared to Onoriode when she was sixteen years old. She told Onoriode many things through the years and they all came to pass. Mother told her that white men would come from a distant land to impose their rule on Ogheli and the surrounding villages.

Onoriode did not understand that dream at the time, but there were so many other dreams that she understood like the one, three years ago, when her mother told her that her husband would have the biggest harvest of yams in Ogheli for five years running, and it happened. She told Onoriode not to worry about her childless marriage. Her mother said she had begged Oghene to give her a few years to play with her grandchildren before letting them into the world. She begged her daughter to be patient. She also gave her daughter a recipe for the dish that will make her husband love her forever. Tonight was the night thought Onoriode, barely containing her excitement. She looked to the sky and spoke to her mother: "Mama, you knew about the Catfish and you kept it to yourself."

That evening went like one of those sweet dreams lubricated by the good hands of providence. The maidens came to help Onoriode prepare the impromptu feast. The young men had refused to go home all day and were working hard at finishing Emerho's supply of palm wine and ogogoro with some degree of success. The top half of the great fish was laid in the centre of the compound, wearing a gloomy expression even for a dead fish. Accolades poured in as people came in one by one to see the spectacle and salute Emerho, the great fisherman. Everyone laughed their collective throats hoarse when Otevwobrise arrived. He stood and looked at the fish for what seemed like an eternity and then slowly shook his head the way one did at the funeral of a great man. People began to convulse in laughter in anticipation of what he would say next for his reputation spoke louder than his words.

"Where are the flies? Why are they not buzzing? Even the usual houseflies in this compound have all stood back in admiration. But where is the tail of the fish?" he smiled with a boyish glint in his eyes as he spoke, extracting great laughter all round. The Ovie was known as a man who liked to tax everything of value in Ogheli. No one liked him. It was a common joke in the village that he went bald at twelve years of age because even his own hair could not stand his greedy personality.

Some giggling girls came over to call the young men to move the fish into the cooking area. When all the yams, plantains, and cocoyams had been peeled and cleaned, the maidens prepared the fish exactly how Onoriode instructed. When it was time to start the actual cooking, Onoriode dismissed all her helpers. They couldn't convince her otherwise. The young girls went to perform their new songs and dances for the young men in the compound. Alone, Onoriode began to cook in the large cooking pots that had been erected on tripods. She moved swiftly from pot to pot, adding spices, tasting with her large spoon, and fanning the waning flames. Soon, a new type of aroma was carried in the dry harmattan air, which drew the maidens back to the cooking area.

"What are you cooking?" they all asked her. She told them to wait. Emerho came over to see what the smell was. "You have excelled yourself. Can I taste some?" he said as he stood by the door of the main kitchen. He twitched his bare chest a few times.

"Be patient," said Onoriode.

"Have you ever seen a patient man before? Please give our hero something to eat. Has he not done the work of twelve men today?" said Osio who lived next door. It was an open secret in the village that Osio, the witch doctor's daughter, wanted Emerho for a husband. They had been friends for a while, but that was before he saw Onoriode dance at a wedding and fell in love with her. Whenever Onoriode teased him about their neighbour, he always said there was no way he would have married a woman who licked spittle with every sentence.

The maidens served the young men while the children gathered in the compound, patiently waiting for Onoriode to feed them. Whenever it was a full moon like tonight, they came to hear stories. Some parents who brought their children also came to have their own bellies filled and ears entertained. When the Ovie made an unexpected appearance at the feast, Onoriode left the children and went to attend to him herself. He was an uncle to Emerho and was a frequent visitor to their house.

"So, what do you call this wonder by the moonlight you have served us?" asked the Ovie as Onoriode knelt before him to clear his leftovers. As no reply was forthcoming, Otevwobrise who was now feeling the effects of too much ogogoro answered, "Ono's food or maybe Emerho's food."

"So what dish is this my daughter, and who taught you how to cook it?' asked the Ovie.

"Ukodo. I call it Ukodo. The recipe was revealed to me in a dream by my late mother," said Onoriode. A wave of murmuring swept through the guests.

"I hope that my stupid second wife is hearing. While she snores like a pregnant vulture, her mates are dreaming of ways to make their husbands happy," said Otevwobrise.

One of the young men reminded him that his second wife had run back to her parents two moons ago after the beating he gave her, following a bout of heavy drinking. He took a large swig of his drink and poured the rest on the floor as a libation to his ancestors. "Drink your own, my fathers, for saving me from that lazy woman," said Otevwobrise.

After the Ovie had left, Onoriode went to the children. She raised a song and they all joined in. The moon shone so brightly that it was possible to see faces clearly without the need for a fire. Soon it was time for what they all came for. One child asked her to show him how Okpufi walks.

"Be patient, young man," she said as she playfully patted his head.

The maidens and the young men crowded around the children to hear the folk tale.

"Once upon a time, in the great distant city of Aka, there lived a great ruler called..."

"Ogiso!" screamed the children.

"And he had a troublesome wife called..."

"Inarhe!" screamed the children who, like fresh palm wine, were now frothing with excitement.

"Story, story," sang Onoriode.

"Story!" screamed the children.

"One morning, Okpufi walked to the palace hungry, and he begged for food. He suffered from yaws and couldn't walk well. Do you want to see how he walked?" she asked.

"Yes!" screamed the kids. The noise attracted more people to the compound.

Onoriode, the clown that she was, did the Okpufi walk. She looked like a duck with piles. People fell on each other in laughter.

"Inarhe refused to give Okpufi any food. She told him to take his diseased legs out of the palace as she was too busy cooking for a visiting Oba and his chiefs. When Ogiso heard that Inarhe had been rude to poor Okpufi, he made her serve him food herself. She got very angry and plotted her revenge," said Onoriode who then paced up and down like someone deep in thought.

"Inarhe plotted and plotted until she got the perfect plan."

"Later that night, when the food was brought out for the feast, the visiting obas and chiefs were very delighted to open up their dishes to find nicely-cooked chicken as the Ogiso had instructed. Inarhe insisted on serving Ogiso herself. She dressed beautifully and danced for Ogiso, calling him by his praise names as she approached where he sat. She knelt down and placed a covered dish before him. When Ogiso opened the dish, he found out that he had the biggest chicken in the whole feast. But do you know what Inarhe had done?"

"No!" the children screamed. Onoriode teased them with that question a few times until Otevwobrise who could take the suspense no more screamed, "Tell us, woman, and put us out of our misery!"

Onoriode reminded him that this story was for the children and continued.

"Ogiso found out that Inarhe had killed a large

chicken and put it in the dish uncooked and with its feathers still on!"

"Never!" screamed some sections of the crowd.

Ogiso became very angry with Inarhe but couldn't say anything because of the important guests present. He told Akwete, the most powerful medicine man in the world to bring the royal calabash. Everyone became scared because the royal calabash contained a Kola nut which only Ogiso could eat. After eating this Kola nut, whatever he said happened. Akwete ran off to the room where the royal crocodile lived. Akwete told the crocodile three times to vomit the royal calabash and it did. When Inarhe saw the calabash which looked bright red as if it had been dipped in blood, she fell on her knees, begging Ogiso to forgive her. Ogiso ate the Kola in silence, and the whole palace fell silent, waiting for him to speak.

He looked at Inarhe and told her that since she had refused to prepare his food, the ancestors would do it. Suddenly, the dead chicken floated out of Ogiso's dish and was suspended in mid-air. One by one, feathers flew out of the chicken, and they all hovered over Inarhe's head. Everyone in the palace was too frightened even to breathe. The next minute, they had to rub their eyes to see if it was really taking place for the chicken began to roast in mid-air without a fire. It was the sweetest smelling roasted chicken they had ever smelt. When the chicken was well-cooked, a tray appeared out of thin air, and the chicken floated onto the tray, which in turn floated to the lap of Ogiso. To teach Inarhe a lesson, Ogiso told the feathers to go into her skin. All her hair fell out, and she was completely covered in feathers for three market days. Throughout this period, she was very nice to everybody.

The audience began to clap wildly. Onoriode milked the applause. "Do you want to know how Inarhe behaved after the feathers fell out?" she asked.

"Yes!" screamed the children.

"Do you want to know if she learnt her lesson?"

"Yes!" screamed the children.

"Then be nice and obedient to your parents, and they will bring you here when next the moon comes out," said Onoriode, finishing with a flourish.

That night, the love cries from Emerho's room were louder than usual. Osio who couldn't sleep had wandered out into the night with her brother Ochuko, and she heard them.

She burned with jealousy, as did her brother.

"What is all the noise about? Is Onoriode the only woman whose husband makes love to her that she has to keep the whole village awake at night?" asked Osio, clapping her hands in feigned wonder.

Ochuko didn't say anything. Every time he looked down at his flabby chest that had no boundary with his abdomen, he shook his head and thought of Ogheli's compound with no fences.

The next morning, the witch doctor, Onogaganmue, had a visit from the Ovie and a powerful witch doctor from Nenerhen called Udumebraye who was renowned in all the neighbouring villages for his wisdom and power. It was to discuss the merits of introducing into Ogheli, the new custom of female circumcision that was spreading throughout the neighbouring villages.

Osio came in to serve the drinks and overheard the conversation. She became gripped by fear for she knew her father very well. He always tried things at home first before going outside.

That night, Osio and her brother, Ochuko, went to see their father in his hut. It was a rectangular mud hut with a thatched roof lit by a small fire, kept going by small twigs which he threw in as he sang to himself. In the corner was a small shrine that stank like an exhumed corpse. Onogaganmue regularly sacrificed pigeons on his personal shrine, and after so many years, he had grown impervious to the smell.

He knew they wanted something. Osio began like a man with an itching sore who scratched the perimeters for hours before finally letting his fingers settle on his intended target. Onogaganmue was always patient with his favourite child.

In the end, she came to the point. "Onoriode is a witch. She stole my husband. Now she has bewitched all the men in the village with her new dish. Why on earth will she not share the recipe with others? I know she cooked that meal with the blood of her unborn children. If I do not become Emerho's second wife, he would go to his grave childless and then what will become…"

"Enough!" shouted Onogaganmue. His children were startled into silence.

After what looked like an eternity, he spoke slowly. "Maybe I should erect a fence, a great boundary between our compound and Emerho's, so that your jealous eyes will stop looking at another woman's husband," said Onogaganmue. Ochuko looked down at his flabby breasts and quivering abdomen when he heard his father mention a boundary. He wondered why the ancestors had given him an ocean for a belly, yet they decided to gift Emerho with small streams with clearly defined banks.

"And you Ochuko, you knew your younger sister was coming to me with this nonsense and you allowed her. Emerho is your age mate. He spends all day planting his yams and very few minutes eating. You spend all day eating and rarely go to work on the few miserable cocoyams you planted." They sat in silence, each one of them afraid to say it loud. They were jealous of their neighbours. "Do not worry. You will not be circumcised first," said Onogaganmue. Osio was beside herself with joy. She thanked her father profusely so much so that he needed a cloth to wipe the spittle from his face.

The next day was like one which had never been seen in the history of Ogheli. All the surrounding villages and towns as far as the great city of Aka heard and retold the story of what transpired that day for many generations. Onogaganmue, fully dressed in his bright red priestly garments, beat a gong and sang maniacally as he made his way to the market square. The town crier ran through the village, summoning all the freeborn citizens of Ogheli for an important meeting. People dashed out of their houses, fearful of bad news. Some wondered if the Ovie had died overnight or perhaps there was a war to fight. At the market place, the mood grew worse when the people saw that over twenty vultures had heeded the call for the meeting and were looking down menacingly from their vantage points atop the sacred Iroko trees. The presence of the Ovie at the gathering and the absence of young men dressed for war heightened the sense of bafflement that cold harmattan morning.

Onogaganmue was straight to the point. The ancestors had appeared to him in a dream and warned of impending danger. A bad omen was on the way. That was because the women in Ogheli were not how they used to be. They no longer respected their husbands as before, and there has been a rise in adultery in the village, causing the gods to close the wombs of some of the daughters of Ogheli and in some cases, making the women have stillborn babies. Onoriode began to feel ill at ease.

"The ancestors in their mercy have said that the danger will be averted," Onogaganmue paused while a huge sigh of relief swept through the crowd. He raised his hands to command silence. "Only if we circumcise that woman there and have her publicly tell us the recipe for her Ukodo," he said, pointing at Onoriode.

From then on, everything blurred into the incomprehensible for Emerho and Onoriode. Onoriode remembered being carried to the home of Onogaganmue by some young men, including Ochuko, who smiled at her despite the terror in her eyes. She shouted out for Emerho to save her but who was he to fight the will of the ancestors?

Onoriode was sick for days afterwards. The whole of Ogheli was sick. Ochuko became depressed and was haunted every night by the screams of pain he heard as he held Onoriode down for the circumcision. The children cried for Ogiso's stories, but no one told them how Onoriode could. The recipe for Ukodo was now common knowledge, but there was a feeling in the village that no one cooked it the way Onoriode had done on that very first night. Onoriode's condition became the new illness in Ogheli, and something had to be done. In the end, the Ovie sent a delegation to Emerho to ask him to throw a big feast and save the town from melancholy.

The next day, the town crier went round the town, saying, "Onoriode, the first daughter of Ogheli who was chosen by the ancestors to bring honour to their town has indeed succeeded in appeasing the ancestors. She would be making an appearance in the market square in seven days." The maidens, however, were all summoned to rally round and meet her every need.

And so it was that the maidens went in to nurse her daily and rub a paste made from camwood on her skin. By noon, they went to the market for fruits, and the market women gave fruits to them for free. Each day, the shopping grew heavier until the young men were needed to help carry the gifts back. Onoriode sent for the children at night to eat the fruits.

On the seventh day, Onoriode looked radiant as she danced through the town in a carnival atmosphere, heading for the market. A little child danced in front of her. On the way back home, Emerho presented a big goat to his in-laws to say thank you for giving him such a blessed wife. That night, they had a feast that surpassed all other feasts that had ever taken place in Ogheli.

Although Osio did not attend, the party spilt over to their compound as Emerho's compound had become too crowded. When the queue for the pit latrine in Emerho's compound became too long, some of his guests started using the one in the Osio's compound, causing her to become angry. She came out of her bedroom completely hysterical and started shouting that the great Onogaganmue's compound was not a public toilet. A fight broke out between Osio and another maiden who happened to beat her severely that she lost an eye.

No one in Ogheli knew exactly who composed the song. It could now be heard at every gathering. The maidens had a dance for it, and they seemed to be infused with extra strength whenever the song was raised.

It is Ukodo tonight,

Finger licking good.

We are doing all right.

I am your woman;

You are my man

Otevwobrise took the credit. He claimed he had started the song on the night the locusts came, just before the planting started. He was at the time worshiping ogogoro, his liquid god with some other ardent worshippers. There was nothing new there. Otevwobrise took credit for many things and was indeed given credit for many things he could not remember doing, such as getting the young Omonigho pregnant. He was forced to marry her as his "second" wife, (seeing that the original second wife ran away and never returned). It was he who started the rumours. White men had been seen in neighbouring villages. No one believed any such thing — that men could be white.

When Onoriode's mother appeared two years later in a dream to tell her about the arrival of her first child, Onoriode was beside herself with joy.

"Give her my name. Call her Ufuoma for she will bring you peace. Whenever you see her, think of me for this is the last time I would be appearing to you," her mother said before fading away like a vapour. Onoriode woke up crying. It seemed one eye poured tears of joy for her unborn child and the other eye mourned for her mother whom she would never see again. Emerho saw things differently. She told him her dream when she served him his breakfast. He smiled and said he had lost his appetite for food. Before Onoriode could ask if there was too much salt in the pepper soup, he led her to his bamboo bed singing.

Today, I shall plant a different seed
For a different harvest,
A harvest of Ufuoma

Shortly after all the planting had been done, on one of the market days, there was an announcement by the town crier for all to assemble at the market square. The message was delivered calmly and provoked no fear in the village. Chief Okpako and Onogaganmue spoke excitedly with each other while Otevwobrise smiled as everyone came over to shake his hand. He was right after all. He had been foretelling the arrival of white men for many moons.

The interpreter introduced the White man who wore funny clothes and spoke in a funny language. The interpreter was a short animated man from Oropke who took great pride in his ability to speak English. Each time he spoke to the White man and turned to speak to the people, he did so with the air of importance of someone who had spoken face to face with Oghene. The white man prayed to an Oghene different from the one known to the people of Ogheli and soon began his preaching. Onoriode came late, walking like she was Okpufi, the poor man in her Ogiso fables whose legs were deformed by yaws. She soon found Emerho and stood next to him. He stroked her now pregnant womb as they listened.

The white man spoke of a God who sent his son to earth. He spoke of many miracles and wonders this messenger performed. The market square was dead silent. Soon the story drifted to the feeding of five thousand people on a mountain.

"What is bread?" asked Otevwobrise. The

interpreter spoke with the white man in hushed tones before announcing that bread was the yam eaten in the white man's land.

"I take it then that your God's messenger made Ukodo on the mountain from five yams and two fishes," said Otevwobrise as he came into the centre of the circle and fixed his eyes on Emerho and Onoriode. The white man was bewildered as to why everyone was laughing.

"My question is, who provided the palm oil?" asked Otevwobrise to great laughter.

"Enough! Keep quiet and let our visitor speak," shouted Chief Okpako.

The white man went on to say that the people killed the messenger who then rose up from the dead in three days.

The man standing behind Emerho spoke aloud to no one in particular, "No group of people can eat Ukodo from Oghene, wipe their mouths clean, and then harm the cook. I don't believe it."

Onoriode had heard enough. He touched Emerho's hands, and he knew it was time to go.

On the way home, he asked why she was crying. She said the baby had just moved. How could she tell him she understood how the messenger from God felt? She had cooked for

Ogheli and the next day, they cut her in her most private place against her will. How would he understand if she told him that her mother had warned her that Ogheli will crumble and its people will become servants to the white man and his many brothers who were to come? How could she voice out her feelings of hatred for the ancestors who had called for her mutilation?

"So what are we going to do tonight?" asked Emerho, abruptly stopping her deep thoughts. He playfully twitched his bare chest as he spoke.

Onoriode stroked her womb and smiled. "I am pregnant already. What more do you want?" she asked gently.

"I want more of you," he said, putting his arm round her shoulder.

"You will get more tonight. I will cook Ukodo for my love," said Onoriode.

This love grows stronger every day;

So fan the flames of a love that just wouldn't die.

Soft music plays as you turn the palm oil

On hot yams so soft and tender.

I will rather be nowhere else, than here

For Ukodo tonight.

Banga Soup Na Love Letter

Write me something tasty
Tell me how you love me
This Delta soul and body
Is hungry, slightly angry

Love, romance, and red flowers
Echo in every chamber
My heart is so in love
And my stomach so in hunger

My gullet groans for the day
My stomach moans for the night
When all will be at peace
When she will get busy with that cooking

I love her sweet perfume
When in a tight embrace
But sometimes I long to sniff
Sweet banga fumes in her hair

Banga ink free-flowing
In starchy fountain pens
Please, write love words on my stomach

That wondrous lovers' den

True love is made in kitchens
Without a care for nails
Condensing a thousand feelings
Into those crafted, lovely dishes

Air freshener is not refreshing
So far from being romantic
Pure banga in the air
Is sweet love and aromatic

My heart's infatuations
Can't trickle to my stomach
If she says she loves me dearly
She better write me something tasty

I sulk, next, it is "what's the matter?"
But how can I explain?
Delta man's love language is so mysterious
Banga soup na love letter

The Glutton's Visit

Happy at departure
Though hungry at arrival
The pot's so empty
Poor host is suicidal

Please, visit no more!
Hospitality annulment!
Poverty on the horizon
He ate down to my last cent

Inviting an elephant disguised as a gazelle?
My hands hold the mountainous blame
He shovelled salt on every morsel
Chewing at speed with no hint of shame

More than food
He ate our joy
Perpetually famished
He nibbled at our dreams

There was no grace in his belches
He criticised all the plans that we told him
I rejoiced to see that guest go
The family now hungry, angry, sad, and slim

KALAKUTA MUSICAL CHOPPINGS

A NIGERIAN MUSICAL ICON THAT DOES NOT make any reference to Naija food, is that one too a Naija musical icon?

Fela's early work set the scene. Jeun ko ku was a song about that glutton who wears out his host with constant visits during mealtimes. At a time when the Nigerian economy was on the rise and many families had disposable incomes with which to show hospitality to visitors, some citizens of our great country were cursed with appetites that exceeded the average host's entertainment budget. Those were the seventies when a walk down a Lagos street meant you sailed through various "smell zones" as you went past each house for there was always a soup being cooked in every kitchen that scented the air. Sometimes, the smells collided in one house as various tenants worked on different recipes. Those in the boys' quarters had pots on stoves also. Depending on which way the wind was blowing, you could smell food from all the geopolitical corners of Nigeria in that Lagos.

Despite the oil boom and abundance of food, some individuals were just too greedy.

Chop and quench
O de
Waki and die
Ode

Forced deportation was in order with strict warnings never to visit again; they had simply overeaten their welcome. This was 1971, and these kamikaze lovers of food risked their lives to get the satisfaction that a stomach stretched to its limits brought. With no fear of high cholesterol, heart attacks or strokes and with complete disregard for diabetes, they bravely ate tunnels through mountains. Gluttony is indeed a disease of plenty. There are no gluttons in famine after all.

Fela called them oni gbese (perennial debtors) for as they have eaten holes in their own pockets, so will they attack other peoples' income with their virulent appetites. But this is Naija, and when we talk about food, we mean Money. Spending money is chopping (eating) money. For visitors wey no sabi, it is politicians "chopping" the National wealth and plunging Nigeria into debt that the groove reminds us of.

In 1972, in Lady, Fela bemoaned the new assertive African woman who, when the table was set, would take meat before anybody, thereby breaking the unwritten rule that the African man must eat meat first (so long as he was not vegetarian). The second rule is that he dies first as too much meat kills but that is another story.

After the reference to ladies came Gentleman in 1973 in which the singer claimed:

> *I no be gentleman at all*
> *I bi Africa man, original*
> *Dem call you, make you come chop*
> *You chop small*
> *You say you belleful*
> *you say you be gentleman*
> *You go hungri, you go suffer, you go quench*
> *mi I no bi gentleman like that*

This was when visitors were still liberally invited to eat due to the relative prosperity of the Oil Boom. Fela poked fun at the African adopting a fake modesty by eating less than he should, while in his mind, he imagines that he is behaving like a gentleman from Europe.

The ruling elite in the seventies took people for granted. The will of the people was trampled underfoot, but the great musician warned in musical parables that the people cannot be treated as enemies as they will always win in the end. The people were likened to water. Easy to use and misuse. Water looks passive, yet it is capable of drowning children. Indeed Water no get enemy (1975)

If you wan cook soup, na water you go use

There is nothing you would do that would not need water.

The heat of the tropics meant the thirst for water was constant. It was the biggest need of the nation. It brought life to us through our mouths. Our bodies are mainly made up of water, so a war declared on water was a stupid war declared on self.

By 1976, things were getting harder for the guys. In the song, No Buredi (Bread), Fela sang:

Hungry dey show im power
You no get power to fight
No buredi

In the subsequent year, the noose on the neck of Nigeria's economy was tightened. In 1977, Fela's Stalemate spoke about the reincarnation of the Jeun Ko ku Glutton albeit the female version:

Two heavy brothers dem sidon inside sun
Dem dey sweat, dem dey share one bottle of beer between dem selves.
Den one fine lady come meet dem, say, "brother, abeg buy mi one bottle of beer na."
Dem go look dem selves
Look the woman

Look dem Pocket
Look dem suffer for Africa
Dem go say stalemate

The heavy brothers probably bought beer by the cartons in previous years, but words fail them now. In addition, and more importantly, their pockets fail them, and they are unable to entertain this Jeun ko ku girl (who interestingly will upgrade to asking for money for Brazilian hair and iPhones in years to come).

By 1981, the chopping, AKA "corruption" had run into overdrive, and the debts stood taller than the great Kilimanjaro. Original Sufferhead was a Fela song that lamented the extinction of the Kamikaze Glutton due to the harsh economic conditions. Everyone was now a longsuffering Naija citizen with chronic malnutrition - an original sufferhead. Men were too hungry to care if the ladies took the meat before them as meat na meat, and you rejoiced when you saw it. The Owambe street parties had dried up, and the family hospitality budget had been eradicated from homes.

Plenty plenty food for Africa
Food underground
Food on the ground
Na so-so plenty food for Africa
Ordinary food for man to chop nko?
E no dey

The scarcity of food was the paradox that Naijaz lived through in the 80s. People felt they were created to suffer due to a curse that had been placed on their heads. The singer articulated the minds and stomachs of the people eloquently:

We all know plenty food for Africa
Plenty plenty land
Plenty fertile land
Plenty plenty farm
Na so so land dey for Africa
Na the big big people dem go dey plant cocoa
If dem no plant cocoa, dem go plant groundnut
Na the big big people go dey plant rubber
Operation feed the nation e plenty well well
Fertiliser scheme dey go and come
Billion billion billion Naira e dey follow am
Now we dey go buy rice from America
We dey make order rice from Brasillia
Dem dey send us rice from Thailand
Green revolution im sef im don start well
Ordinary food for men to chop for town nko?
E no dey

The importation of rice continues to shame the nation long after the singer had died and gone. The music continues to be played and the Jollof rice continues to be eaten. There is a prophetic dimension to music made by the great singers of the past.

Today's musicians will not let us rest with their plenty plenty banana and so so big cassava o!!!

And the hunger continues.

HUNGER

Hunger starts off politely. it greets you with an early morning hug and a kiss which is soon followed by nastiness if food does not appear. Man muss wack after all. The older people resort to lamentations and philosophies when hunger pangs strike them at a time their fridges and pockets are empty, but the babies have not read that memo. They just cry, making sounds designed to go straight to the brain of an adult and propel them to action. When parents feel impotent in the face of hunger, frustration rises and actions become unpredictable. In the midst of the painful hunger, the adults get that epiphany of torment in their minds: someone somewhere in this town has enough leftovers to feed my family.

People will procrastinate if they can get away with it, so nature makes sure there is no opportunity to, "forget to eat" or "forget to feed the baby." The world stops until food goes into the mouth. Various countries quote between 20 to 40% of household food that goes to waste. That is not adding the percentage of farm produce that rots away after harvest or gets intentionally burnt so as not to flood the market with food and upset the price structure.

"In the abundance of water, the fool is thirsty," says Bob Marley, but the hungry may disagree. They do not have access to food. They are not so foolish as not to know they are hungry and neither are they so dumb that they cannot guess which part of town has well-stocked fridges. They are wise enough to know that they cannot just turn up at a house and bang on the gates asking to be let in so that they could have dinner with the rich guys. Na today?

There was a rich man who was dressed in purple and fine linen and lived in luxury every day. At his gate was a beggar named Lazarus, covered with sores and longing to eat what fell from the rich man's table. Even the dogs came and licked his sores.

Hunger can get so bad that people could migrate their homes to live illegally outside the gates of the rich in expectation of a few crumbs. This new location guarantees nothing as the parable told by Jesus clearly shows. Death comes to take away the starving beggar on a chariot with space for two. The rich man too is taken, but the food is left behind.

Hunger was meant to be a beautiful thing. It is the gentlest reminder that it is time to eat. This prevents people from wasting away. People always need to be reminded to do things, even paying the bills for what they have purchased. The gentle reminder is always followed by the bailiffs who come looking for the property they can confiscate. Hunger has its own metabolic bailiffs that eat away at the body's stored-fat if there is no food in the stomach. This is a painful process, and the individual starts to lose weight.

The world of leftovers is a strange one. Humans work so hard for food then throw it away. Chop remain is what the village people call it. There is a stigma attached to eating the leftovers of others, but when hunger catches you, all stigmas are forgotten. Hunger is democratised in Nigeria. The boys of Bornu state experience it in the same way the girls in Calabar do. Once that fire burns, all tribes do the same thing, which is to choose food to douse the flames and pangs. For the hungry lad in Borno who prefers to eat his own type of food, preferences melt like wax under the thermal glory of hunger. Anything will do, from the amala and ewedu of the West to the Afang soup of the East, he go rush dem. Apart from the catching, Nigerian hunger sometimes joins forces with the hot sun and greedy mosquitoes to beat Nigerians. Hunger beating you is both a physical, psychological and spiritual abuse. The lashes are lavish, and they make the victim cry out loud (usually to God), asking why they were born in this country and why their parents no get moni. Next comes the raining of curses on the heads and graves of everyone who has ruled Nigeria till date. The lashing intensifies despite the cries.

Suddenly, the object of the hungry man's hatred turns up and throws some banknotes at him and he smiles, grabs the money, and runs off to buy eba so that belle go gauge. It is election time after all.

It is impossible to discuss national hunger without a mention of ppolitics and lleadership because agricultural policies and investments lie in the hands of the government and those Civil Servants that should be serving the hungry with plates of food. Anyone in charge of a local government area, state or country should no longer feel at ease when they are in possession of the information that there are citizens under their watch going to bed hungry; that is falling off to sleep on empty stomachs, fridges, and wallets. Just what is the prestige of presiding over starving people whose brains are being burnt up for metabolic fuel? Where would national development come from when the people are in survival mode?

A fifteen-car procession of a governor speeding past hungry Africans on the way to the airport is an absurd curse rather than a prestigious show of strength. It is like meeting a finely dressed man on the streets with a $40,000 watch while his kids are crying for bread at home. It would be impossible to respect such a father. The truth of the matter is that the leader of the starving is really starving, no matter how much he has in his wallet. The people may be starved of food and dignity, but the leader is starved of his humanity. Ask the leader about this, and he would reply, "Did they tell you my children are starving?"

Second bass jare!

Body Fat for Dinner

Raindrops travel a great distance
Pregnant with messages
The earth is now fertile
The harvest will arise with joy

Indoors, he gets his own message
Drops expose a leaky roof
He moved the pans to catch the drops
He felt less than a man

Half a man and half a soul
He made the announcement with shame
and great sorrow
Hungry eyes listened in despair
Their body fat was for supper tonight
They looked at mama who looked away
They looked at their bony bodies
And they saw no fat
He felt half a father

The rains came harder

On the house of the pauper
A loving man but tonight, not a provider
He bit his lip and cried in silence
No food tonight for all
Except the foetus in her belly
There was a strange smell in the air
That perfume death wears on hungry cold nights

The frying from miles away
Made it to their nostrils
They had nothing to chew
And nothing to suck
No need for toothpicks
There was nothing stuck
Early to bed and the mosquitoes were joyful
Fresh blood for dinner tonight

Empty Vessel

The machine is alive
But its tanks are empty
We drove for three hours
And passed an ocean of plants
Yet the government says there is no food
To power my machine
So how does grass grow
Where food cannot grow?

The brains all stopped working
Fine solar panels in dark caves
The creativity is starving
A generator of ideas without the diesel
No fuel no movement
No food no development
Mosquitoes say I'm edible
But I'm an empty vessel

The starving too have ideas
It is all about the food.
The hungry have big stomachs

That pine for food and drink
With trillions of seeds around
The pot is an empty vessel
With some much desire for milk
The stomach stays an empty vessel

Fridge Vacancy

A position to fill
But no one seems interested
A white clean office
Air-conditioned and well-lit
Incoming trays are empty
In anticipation of goodness.
The month has finally ended
But the vacancy remains

I peep through the doors
To embrace that vacant expression
Of emptiness and want
Its penury's storefront
My fridge, my mirror
My reflection, my life
In a world of a trillion fruits
Not one has occupied mine

No eggs no bread
No milk or butter to spread
White supremacy? White everywhere

A rainbow-coloured fridge
To douse this hunger monotony
It is not a fridge but a morgue
The vacant enclave is
Death kept fresh, kept cold

Nothing Else

I have XYZ and nothing else
A clean white plate and nothing else
The raging appetite so wondrous
The redundant cutlery so ominous
I dreamt of frothing okra embedded with dried fish
But I swallow spit as the sun rises
A healthy appetite and infirm pockets
Weigh out my hope
So many certificates
But nothing else

Cutlery arrayed for battle
But nothing else
Pots and pans for show
It's a museum in a faraway land
I am spiritual
I fast and pray but break the fasting
With salty tears.
I have water to water my hands
But nothing else

I have an empty stomach
But nothing else

I am blessed with teeth
But nothing else to show
I could crunch bone to powder
Then wash down with gulder
A sense of smell so heightened
I smell hot dodo frying in distant streets
Great talent for eating
But nothing else to show

AGEGE BREAD OF LIFE

IF THE HOLY LAND HAD BEEN SITUATED IN Lagos, Nigeria, then the first four Books of the New Testament collectively called the Gospels would have been named differently. The Books of Mudiaga, Maduka, Lamido, and Jesutosin would have reflected the local population and Jesutosin Chapter 6 Verse 35 would read "I am the Agege Bread of Life."[1]

There are so many references to food and drink in the Bible, and bread features heavily. This is proof that there can be no spirituality without food. The multiple mentions of fasting clearly tell us that the temporary abstinence from food is not a hunger strike. There is always an end to a fast. The state where human beings live on calorie deficient or poor diets goes against the Christian faith. Ending world hunger is a goal. It is a shame, but many hungry people still find it necessary to ask that legitimate question, "Who prayer epp?"

15 Suppose a brother or a sister is without clothes and daily food. 16 If one of you says to them, "Go in

peace; keep warm and well-fed," but does nothing about their physical needs, what good is it?

The starving man has been in prayer for days hoping to encounter a plate of nice edible food, and it can be such a disappointment for the hungry to stumble across someone who thinks they know how to pray away the hunger pangs they have not felt. The cure for hunger is food, and hunger is one of the certainties of life.

Food is a spiritual substance that has great powers of healing the soul and body. A full stomach frees the body from the constraints that hunger and scarcity put on the brain. All great nations have the majority of their population eating food on a regular basis. This needs planning, and God knows this. A lot of the Bible talks about seedtime and harvest time. In the absence of a famine, there should be food for all for it is common knowledge that you plant seeds in the planting season in hope of a subsequent harvest. This is how the planet has been from its inception, so it is no surprise that people are hungry and in need of food when the right seeds are not sown.

Likewise, it is simple to deduce that you plant enough food for the population you have. The need to resort to food importation is unpardonable. Through the ages, planting seasons and harvest seasons have been celebrated with rites and feasts. Seeds must be sown for it is suicidal not to. Those who do not sow will starve in harvest time.

Jesus is the bread of life. Bread is king. Milk must be queen. Why was that bread metaphor used? The truth is that food is life. Most of what we do as human beings only occur after eating well. Someone once told me I took food too seriously, and this was somehow wrong. Well, he had a full fridge to start with, so how would he know the importance of food when he has never seen a kwashiorkor patient before? I was shaken to my foundations when I saw a kwashiorkor patient as a medical student in Nigeria. I found it hard to believe there were malnourished children in Benin City at the time because all the people I knew were eating regularly. The well-fed should have some alimentary compassion for their brothers.

The Bible has Adam and Eve eating what they were not supposed to and being evicted from the Garden of Eden. One of their children killed his brother after harvest time because he was jealous of God's acceptance of his brother's sacrifice. Further along, Esau sold his birth right to his brother, Jacob, for a pot of food. The greatest turnaround in fortunes came by way of Joseph who went from the prison to the palace because he knew the blueprint for effective food management in Egypt for the next fourteen years. This was food management at a national scale — storing grain without the benefits of electricity throughout the first seven years of a bumper harvest and the later seven years of famine.

It is strange that in today's world with cold storage and computerisation, nations cannot produce enough beans to feed the people. Prophet Elisha asked for a pot of stew to be cooked, but a "learner" picked the wrong herbs, and it became death-in-a-pot. Elisha sprinkled in flour and the pot was miraculously healed. God's plan is that his people must eat.

Soon after, someone brought twenty loaves of bread which he shared among one hundred men and had leftovers due to a miraculous bread multiplication. Miraculous food must have tasted divine. Jesus showed he cared about the state of people's stomach by miraculously feeding five thousand hungry people and saving the all-night prayers for Himself. Satan tempted Him with a stone-to-bread conversion temptation, but He saw through it. The fast was due to end.

His first miracle, a water-to-wine conversion thrilled wedding guests, and He also blessed Peter with so much fish that his net almost broke. The Old Testament had the Passover, a hastily eaten meal on the last night in Egypt, and the New Testament has a mirror image of Passover meal popularly called the Last Supper. The bread and wine eaten represented Jesus' body and blood respectively.

The longest feeding plan was, however, the feeding of over one million Jews in the desert for forty years with manna from heaven. Out of the slavery from Egypt, through the wilderness into the Promised Land flowing with milk and honey: that was God's Plan. Beyond eating food is the enjoyment of the eating process. The gratitude one gets for having a slice of bread is spiritual. The joy that comes from swallowing chewed food is not experienced by all. It is a gift from God. Man has no other duty than to eat his food with relish and gratitude and praise to God for the privilege.

> A person can do nothing better than to eat and drink and find satisfaction in their own toil. This too, I see, is from the hand of God,
>
> for without him, who can eat or find enjoyment? To the person who pleases him, God gives wisdom, knowledge and happiness, but to the sinner he gives the task of gathering and storing up wealth to hand it over to the one who pleases

God. This too is meaningless, a chasing after the wind.[2]

Some might not believe that we are here to eat and be merry. They think like poets all day long and soon get depressed. The aim of all living being has to be the service to our fellow men, feeding them with love and support and expressing thanks and praise to our creator. What, you may ask, about those who do not believe in God? Well, no one is exempt. Everybody must be the Agege bread of life to their neighbour.

References

1.   James 2:15–16 (NIV)

2.   Ecclesiastes 2:24–26 (NIV)

THE DEATH OF A TOASTER

AFTER EIGHT YEARS OF SERVICE, I REGRET TO announce the death of my toaster. It has served my family well; a dedication to service exemplified by the six thousand nine hundred slices of bread that have passed through its hot bowels for onward transport to our bowels.

A life not examined is not worth living. I have reflected on our relationship and found my toaster to be that faithful friend. You burnt my toast just sixteen times. That compared to my forty-six times of being unfaithful is my biggest regret.

I left you at home while I took holidays to Europe to enjoy Spanish, Cypriot, and French toasters and foreign breads. I recall, with relish, the Oriental Hotel in Lagos where the toaster was a conveyor belt arrangement. Slice bread in and toast out at the other end. How could I ever leave you lonely and fly away to sunny West Africa to have my bread toasted by another?

I apologise but have no sweet or soothing words to say save repeating what the King said:

Maybe I didn't treat you
Quite as good as I should have
Maybe I didn't love you
Quite as often as I could have
Little things I should have said and done
I just never took the time
You were always on my mind
You were always on my mind

Even now, you are on my mind. The Titanic has sunk, but our love will always go on.

Take no offence in the fact that I have already replaced you. You know these children. They wake up demanding toast without a care for your life work or your meritorious service to this family. No loyalty. Kids! You would love your replacement though. White, shiny and should I say, beautiful? Do not get me wrong. You are still the finest like my S.O.S people would say.

After all that we've been through,
Time won't change the way I feel about you.
Out of all the loves before,
You're the finest I've ever known.

Alas! They say that the best thing since sliced bread is the toaster and who am I to disagree? We have been through a lot. I recall that summer in 2010 when I brought you back to an empty house. You had pride of place in my kitchen. I played It's my house by Diana Ross to welcome you, and that first toast was divine. I recall the butter, taste, and texture of the bread. Though you couldn't eat, you watched me lovingly while I ate. All manner of bread slices went through you over the years. Your handling of the Hovis and Warburton's brands was legendary although Agege Bread never seemed to sit well with you. (Abi you be racist?)

The ability to take a moderately desirable slice and turn it into a "hot" item is probably why suitors are called "toasters" in Lagos. There is hardly a fine girl who has been able to maintain the same weight, financial strength or levels of stress after succumbing to the life-transforming enticements of a suitor. Yes o! Toasters change lives.

There is no toast bread that can reverse the toasting process and return to its original state — the pure 'today's bread' state all wrapped up in see-through polythene coverings. Once browned off, there is no going back. So you see, my dead electrical appliance, as a man toasts his babe, so did you toast my bread with a beautiful transformational agenda.

Eight years is quite long, but I had hoped for twenty

years. That was why I did not agree to an insurance policy when I bought you (Almost like a pre-nuptial agreement for toasters sef). There has been no power surge in my neighbourhood before, and your longevity was never threatened. I was sure I would use you past the guarantee date.

I have a friend in Lagos who has complained about losing electrical appliances due to electric current fluctuations. Fans, fridges, and air conditioners banished to premature electrical purgatory without compensation being paid by the electric power holding companies.

You have witnessed the arrival of the children and played host to many visitors. You did your work behind the scenes with aplomb. Your two-slices-of-bread capacity was never a problem. For you, we waited. Through various World Cups Finals, Christmases, New Years, winters and summers, we have been together.

No loss of appliance has hit me this bad before. Well, except for my chassis electric kettle that was stolen off me during the first week of A Levels at Zambesi House at FGC, Kaduna. It still hurts even now. The thief may see me tomorrow and start hugging me like a long lost old school friend. I digress.

All good things must end. So, off I go to the recycling cemetery to dump you. May your elements rest in peace. "No Orchids for Miss Blandish," James Hadley Chase wrote. That fate is yours. You have no grave, no tombstone, no flowers, nothing but precious memories.

I need to channel some Warri investigative journalism now before the final goodbye.

Oh, great toast of the town now in the land of your ancestors! Was anyone involved in your death? Were you poisoned or sabotaged? We have heard of those Street Light Interference (SLI) people that can turn off lights just by walking past them. Na SLI people wound you? I am going to review all my WhatsApp and telephone messages. Anyone who messaged me before your time of death has Ogbanje spirit, and I will block them from my life before they wreck more appliances.

All the best, my good friend. Let's take consolation from Amy Grant. We would meet again one day.

In a little while,
We'll be with the father
Can't you see him smile? (Oh)
In a little while
We'll be home forever
In a while

We're just here to learn to love him
We'll be home in just a little while

Sorry, I made an error. No toast in heaven. Anyway, I am off now. Been called down for breakfast, and I can smell the toast.

GHANAIAN JOLLOF RICE

A GREAT SAGA IS SOMETIMES INSTIGATED BY a tiny spark such as an errand.

When faced with self-afflicted calamitous episode, the Naija man must, in the spirit of self-examination, ask himself the question, "Na who send me message?"

Nothing propels you forward in life like an errand. Goliath lost his head on the back of this errand. Now, Jesse said to his son, David, "Take this ephah of roasted grain and these ten loaves of bread for your brothers and hurry to their camp. And the world talks about David and Goliath situations till today.

And so I got a text message at work, "Please, can you collect Joel's gift and some food from Mary's place on the way back from work?"

The answer is always yes to these requests. I recall a friend who was asked to help pick up something on his way home from work at his wife's parents' Kaduna home. The only problem was that he lived and worked in Abuja. When he protested that Kaduna was not on the way home, he was told, "Go and see what your mates are doing for their wives." I digress.

Show me your errands, and I will tell you who you are. The errands maketh the man after all. The lonely have no one to send them anywhere. Those with company do errands all day. I digress again.

Anyway, I appeared at Mary's house, and I was sent on my way with my son's birthday present and a container of Ghanaian jollof rice. I did not ask who the rice was for as I assumed the women had discussed ownership rights of the said jollof.

As I drove home, the aroma from the rice filled the car and did strange things to my brain. Alone with a rice that smelt like it came from heaven, I started to get adulterated flashbacks to history lessons of yore. Did Chief Priest Okomfo Anokye conjure, from the skies, a golden bowl of Ghanaian jollof rice for the first Asantehene of the Asante Kingdom, His Royal Highness Osei Tutu? Or was it just the golden stool he brought down from the skies?

The more I drove, the more I thought of parking the car in front of one of these shops along the way home that sold plastic containers so I could divide the rice into two and leave my own in the car to be retrieved later in the night when all have slept.

The next idea that formed was to elope with the rice to France for two days. By the time my worried family reports me missing to the police and go through the stress of searching for me, they would have forgotten the rice when I turn up with a tale of having been abducted by kidnappers and almost sacrificed in a money ritual (too much Nollywood abi?).

You see, food is a powerful thing in the presence of hunger. Diverse temptations and creative lies abound in the mind of the possessor of an empty stomach. Some might wonder why a Nigerian is being tortured by a foreign jollof when we have our own version. Time and chance, my people, time and chance.

Apart from errands, a man is also made by the gifts bestowed upon him. On the said day, my wife was gifted with Ghanaian jollof, and that was my experience. Perhaps, if I was gifted with Nigerian jollof, this article would have turned out different. And yes, I have eaten Nigerian jollof before, complete with dodo, moin-moin, gizzard, and beef. However, the past meals mean nothing when you are famished and you are faced with a hot meal within reach. (A jollof in hand is worth thirty in the Hippocampus' memory bank).

How could I write of Cameroun Jollof embellished with coconut oil or the Liberian or Sierra Leone versions? Togo and Republic of Benin have their own jollof as does the Senegalese Wolof Jollof popularly called "one pot" and said to be the first Jollof ever made. No nationals from these West African countries called me to collect a "take-away". So, on this day, it was Ghana alone that gave me independence from hunger.

Oh yes! I recall the Nigerian Jollof of my youth. However, the CV of past meals can never give comfort when a man is famished. If you doubt this, ask Esau when you die so he can tell you how he sold his birth right and destiny for a plate of food.

By the time I was parking my car, good conscience and common sense had prevailed, and I decided to present the items to my wife without any taxation.

I asked tentatively, "Who did Mary do this rice

for?" And she answered, "It is for us na. Why do you ask?"

I heaved a hidden sigh of relief. Later, I muttered, "Oh, I thought you made a special request. I might eat a bit."

On the table, I did pray a prayer of thanksgiving for the meal which had to be cut short as my mouth flooded with saliva. It felt like the Volta River had sprung forth in my mouth while my lips acted as the Akosombo Dam. Those acquainted with the Pavlov's experiments will catch my drift.

The meal took place at night, and my two-year-old son hustled hard for a good share of the Ghanaian Jollof. Despite it being dark outside, in the words of Osibisa, it was a "sunshine day" on our dinner table. Pure Black Star tinz.

FOOD AND I

THEY SAY THAT THE WAY TO A MAN'S heart is a tale of two cardiologists. The hospital cardiologist travels via femoral artery in the groin or the radial artery at the wrist to arrive at the heart using tubes and radiological equipment.

The lady in the kitchen, also a cardiologist of sorts and perhaps an "other room practitioner" gets to the heart through her soup laden with poly-saturated fatty acids. This fat travels via the stomach to block off the coronary arteries leading to "death by brief illness" as they say in Nigeria. What a woman can do, a man can do also. There are male cardiologists in the kitchens of this world cooking up slow poison.

Food is beautiful and there are many beautiful things that can kill, but let us move on from terra-depression to terra-happy. I love food, and by the grace of God, it will not kill me either through the fast or slow poisons contained therein. Food is such an iconic necessity that lends itself so generously to literature. In the novel Things Fall Apart by Chinua Achebe, yams are portrayed as Alpha male tubers symbolising wealth and power. Who can forget Chapter Five with its tale of a wealthy man celebrating the Feast of the New Yam with what can best be described as a Trump Tower of foo-foo. The mound was so high that relatives who sat on opposite sides only saw each other when the "mountain" had been levelled, aided and abetted by vegetable soup.

Charles Dickens' Oliver Twist asked for more and was punished for his audacity. This story strikes a chord with all for the request for an extra helping is universal, especially at the table of a skilful chef.

Unfortunately, some children in the world are not fortunate to have a tiny first course not to talk of having jara. Many parts of Africa are in famine. It is sad that the neighbouring countries cannot help. Africa looks to the West for help when these things happen. One does wonder if these African countries have supplies of grain to last them at least a year. If they don't, they should. Without electricity, grain was stored for seven years in

Egypt during a famine according to the Bible. This was ancient Africa. In today's world, one should expect hunger to have been eradicated by now.

The thought of a child going to bed hungry is heart breaking, especially when there are no wars to blame. Growing maize and rearing goats and chickens are simple matters. Piping water from the sea or local rivers is also a simple matter.

The Nubian Sandstone Aquifer System is an ocean far underground, spanning Libya, Egypt, Sudan, and Chad. Discovered in Libya in 1953 while prospecting for oil, this reserve of fresh water was exploited by Muammar Gaddafi via the Great Man Made River project in 1991. It sounds incredulous that the eastern part of the Sahara desert has water underneath it.

This is just one example of how water can be piped across vast geographical areas to provide water for irrigation for farms. Bad weather has been going on since time began, and governments should plan for it. Countries that import food and have no stored grain or water supplies are disasters waiting to happen. And when the inevitable drought happens, the children die first.

The two African leaders with lofty and ambitious ideas in recent times have been

Muammar Gaddafi of Libya and Thomas Sankara of Burkina Faso, and they are both dead. Both had firm plans for agriculture. Ironically, the leaders in Africa with no long-term plans, who just roll over and let the multinationals rape the land, tend to live very long.

I still love my food. West Africa grows cocoa and imports chocolate bars, yet I still love my African food. I have been blessed never to have lived in an area of food shortage throughout my life. I see people who run away from food because they want to lose weight, yet in some corners of the world, people go hungry. When one person starves, we all starve as human beings.

Ukodo is a meal I enjoy. It is one from Urhobo land, and it conjures memories of childhood and family. It is strongly linked to my identity as an Urhobo man so much that I wrote a poem about it entitled Ukodo Tonight. Eating together round a table is good for family life, and at the table, kids get reminded that they are part of something important.

Good affordable food and water are fundamental human rights.

(Epp us share di Gala)

THE TABLE MATTERS

PREVENTION IS MIGHTIER THAN THE CURE and less expensive. Many psychological ailments that plague us in adulthood could have been immunised against during childhood by simply having a roundtable conference with food at the centre.

From the glutinous date, who eats up all her starter and then eyes yours, to the greedy local government chairman high on drugs and pilfered wealth, we see people whose problems could have been prevented by eating regular family dinners.

No one in folklore history needed family dinners, and the training it dispenses like the tortoise that broke his shell in Chapter 11 of Chinua Achebe's Things Fall Apart. As the story goes, the birds were invited for a feast in the sky and seeing that helicopters had not been invented, the only way Mr Tortoise could gate-crash the party was to borrow a Personal Flying Card (PFC) from each bird. He had a reputation for mischief, but he talked them into giving him a one-bird-one-feather loan.

During the flight to the party, he assumed the alias, "All of You", and as soon as their hosts presented food for "All of You", the Tortoise stepped in to display his greed. The angry birds withdrew their support. So, by the end of the party, he was filled with food but could no longer hum his favourite R. Kelly tune.

The parrot offered to tell his wife to put out soft furniture in the garden for his proposed wingless jump back to earth. The parrot, however, told Mrs Tortoise to bring out metallic objects. Alas, Mr Tortoise jumped. The impact took the 's' out of his shell (proof that when the people get angry with the leader they helped to send flying upwards and withdraw their support, a painful crash is inevitable).

If the Tortoise had spent time with his parents at the dinner table, he would have learnt the following essential lessons:

- **Curb the Greed**

Being reprimanded for an attempt to grab the chicken without consideration for the rest of the family, especially at an early age, leaves indelible marks on the personality.

- **Realise that all at the table must have equal opportunities**

The bread comes round and no one takes a lion share. Equitable distribution of food according to need is learnt and practiced.

- **There is always a next meal**

Spoiling breakfast endangers lunch. If the food is too salty at lunch, you may not want to endanger your chances of dinner by talking out of turn or hurting the cook's feelings

- **Never bite the finger that feeds**

The head of the table that pays the bills blesses the food and generally steers the ship. Things get done in the correct order and every one's space is respected. No one reaches across the next man's face to grab the salt but rather asks politely if they could pass it. That is how personal space is learnt — to be respected — and this translates into respect for international boundaries later in life.

- **There is life after the meal**

Those who have stayed behind to talk and laugh, after the meal has long finished, know that communication with family members must still go on, and it is an enjoyable part of the post-dinner experience. Being greedy and eating all the rice will breed resentment and disharmony. That is why many people who are rich through greedy means are paranoid and always watch their backs for they know there is no goodwill coming from any quarters.

- **The table is for service**

You serve those you live and eat with (not defraud them). At home, you learn to do the noble act of setting the table for others (even God prepared a table in Psalm 23). Setting a table is forward-planning. Each seat is allocated to someone, and they grow up knowing that there is a special place reserved for them. Eating meals in harmony during childhood will produce civil servants rather than the civil merchants on the lookout for a bribe.

The tortoise was helped to the sky, but he soon forgot his helpers. The 1971 song by the then Fela Ransome-Kuti called Jeun Ko Ku (Chop and Quench), seems most appropriate to tell about the Tortoise's expulsion from the party in the sky.

In the song, Jeun Ko Ku, the singer laments being saddled with a greedy visitor who eats up the whole economy and even makes passes at the lady of the house. He calls the visitor, "oni gbese" (a debtor) for eating recklessly above his means. Greedy children without reins on their appetites grow up to be greedy leaders who "eat up" the economies they were given feathers to fly into. They soar on the mandate of the people but build far-away nests for themselves in which they hide all their looted funds. Fela cried for help to expel the visitor who is hell-bent on eating to the point of achieving a stomach rupture.

So, the next time a cunny orator asks for something you have that would enable him get to a position of power, look him in the eyes and ascertain if he ate meals with his parents or was a hustler with a survival instinct and an eye for looting. If he appears to be a crook, keep your feathers to yourself.

NAIJA HANDWORK

EVERY NAIJA IS A FOOD-HANDLER, FROM THE infants on a breast milk diet to the grandees demolishing mountains of Tuwo with aplomb. Those who know what they want don't waste time answering questions in a buka.

"Swallow or non-swallow?" They blink their answer.

"Cutlery or hand?" They laugh and walk over to their usual seat, saying, "Before nko?" without looking back. Mama Put should know by now is what they infer.

The interaction between the chef and the hungry is like one of those rites you watch on the Discovery Channel. People behave differently when they smell the aroma of food. There is a good reason to take people who you want to do business with out for a meal first. While it is good to see people under pressure, it is also more important to see them under pleasure.

Some Naija people, guys especially, take off their jackets, undo the cuff links and the belt in anticipation of incoming pounded yam and ogbono soup. They get very universally receptive to all pleasures once the mouth is assured of traffic. Pure Blood Group AB abi?

On the roads, traffic is controlled digitally through traffic lights made from metallic materials while in some countries, traffic wardens direct cars manually using hand signals. On the dining table, there are cutleries which are modern and easily cleaned and still, some opt to eat with their fingers.

The question is, why direct food into your mouth with your hands when the clean utensils are present?

I must have been about six when we visited a family friend and found them eating eba and soup with their cutlery. I recall laughing at the incredulous activity with my sister. It did not stop there for we went home and told everyone what we had seen.

People commented on how the food would not taste nice and wondered what craziness had possessed these poor ajebutas. A bit silly in retrospect, but that was how I was then. This premise of food not tasting as well when eaten with a fork and knife is akin to saying a Bentley would not drive well across a junction if it was directed by traffic lights as opposed to a traffic warden standing in the middle of the road, waving people along with his hands.

It could be said, however, that eating with the hand has advantages as the fingers are indeed sensitive probes. The texture of the food is felt, the temperature of the food can be ascertained, and there is no risk of sneezing and stabbing your lips with a fork.

I, however, changed from a garri-handler i.e., eating with my fingers to being a fork-and-knife guy as time progressed. Not for any particular reasons other than choice and not wanting soup on my fingers. Ironically, that is the same reason some give for wanting to eat with their hands — the satisfaction derived from licking soup off the fingers.

Growing up, garri was a friend. One was involved in a warm handshake with that cassava product most days. Eba even doubled up as paper glue when kites were being constructed or postage stamps refused to adhere to envelopes. We change as we grow. I think surgical training must have reset my brain. In theatre, you "scrubbed up" before every case, and you brushed away at the hands, making sure no inch of skin was missed. The nails were kept short and had extra attention under the running water. Once the hands are dried, the next stop is the table where the patient waits, unconscious, for your clean hands and sharp instruments.

The knowledge that bacteria lie everywhere gets drummed in. Your hands touch nothing else once washed and gloved. Over time, one began to approach every table with that same routine — thoroughly washed hands that held clean instruments. Even though the plate of food belongs to an individual, they are still responsible for making sure that the plate always has some semblance of civility during the course of the meal so as not to repulse others. Deft and gentle moments would make sure the food on the plate always looks like the leftovers of a human being and not a wolf.

Unfortunately, there seems to be little dining etiquette in Naija dinner table culture especially with swallows. It is just a case of, wash the hand, bless the food, and then speedily subject the food to a humiliating public execution.

The washing of the hand varies. I have seen people submerge their right hand (always the right) in a bowl of water like a kind of prompt water baptism and rush on to eat. The bacteria might become wet by this manoeuvre, but they remain on the hand.

Watching some eat their pounded yam and ogbono can be comical so long as you do not have the displeasure of eating opposite them. Once the hand is baptised, it approaches the mound of pounded yam usually from the south east position and a corner is pinched off, somewhat like the then annexation of the Bakassi peninsular. The neck is tilted to the left during this action.

Then the lump of poundo is then moulded in the palm till perfectly spherical and suddenly indented in its equator without splitting it into two (like an ancient hour glass). Now comes the bit which should be done only at home. The pounded yam approaches the soup with the food-handler leaning forward like he needs to see the soup but is longsighted. Just before the pounded yam strikes the surface of the soup, the mouth slowly opens with the tongue stuck out as if the tip of the tongue is aiming for the chin. By the time the pounded yam is smeared in soup and upward bound, the mouth widens up to six times the diameter of the bolus of pounded yam. Rather than swallowing the stuff and save everybody a clear view of the excessive salivation, tonsils, and uvula, the food-handler starts to rotate the slimy bolus of food to disentangle it from dripping soup that may stain the shirt. The mouth remains wide still. Next, the mouth is brought closer to the hand and young children begin to fear they might get swallowed. The food goes in, but this is not the end.

The sound effects start. Licking, sucking, and wanton exhibitions of relish followed by an exclamation of how "this soup sweet o!"

The remaining half of the pounded yam soon dives in for soup and the cycle continues. It is a free world, but why do this outside private residences? Some meticulous people eat with their hands, and they are like a noiseless Bentley, moving beautifully and irritating nobody.

Others are in a feeding frenzy, even taking their first cut of the pounded yam from the summit and staining the rest of the mountain with soup. (Now, who climbs a mountain starting at the top?) With soup dripping down their lips and down to the elbows, they have the temerity to tell you with a mouth full of half masticated meat blended with ogbono, "You meet me well bros, come chop."

The answer is standard in Nigeria, "Thanks bros, but I just had something."

CROWD CHOPPING

CROWD-CHOPPING IS THE CONSUMPTION OF a vast amount of food by many participants who each contribute their appetites and stomach volumes to the cause. Some come with healthy appetites while others come equipped with greed but in the end, the job gets done. My thoughts are inclined to two extremes on the spectrum of chopping. At one end, is it the one-man-one-plate arrangement AKA, "*One man one Machete*" by TM Aluko or at the other end, is a group around the plate also known as *Man-of-the-people* arrangement by Prof. Chinua Achebe.

Proponents of communal eating warn those who eat alone by citing the dreaded *eat alone and die alone* adage. This saying is guaranteed to make a superstitious Naija person share what they have. I am all for sharing, but I no more like sharing plates with people the way I used to do.

Nigerians are great believers in sharing food. Even before the food is fully cooked, we love to stare at food in groups and just drool. I have watched Nigerians queue for food at parties and at Bukas, and it is always the same. All phones off, glasses on, and everyone just stares longingly. Even great proselytes who claim that they walk by faith and not by sight find their resolve weakened at the sight of a pot of steaming Jollof rice. Not only do they stare as one hypnotised, but they also develop laser-sharp focus on the food.

There are places on the streets at night where you find Naijaz zombified, gazing longingly at the Suya man's grill, by the mama's hot oil pot in the street corner, frying yams, dodo, and akara, and at the local Mama Put where the whole queue stretches their necks as those in front of them are served from the pot of stew. MamaPuts are bizarre. The Mama spreads her legs apart with the pot of stew in front of her, and she holds the plate of the customer.

"Which meat you want?"

Strange but true, and the customer points at a piece of meat. How is the choice made?

Sometimes, it takes ages to get that particular piece centred on the spoon and transferred to the plate under watchful eyes. A sense of unity and bonding forms among all those who eat from the same pot. No wonder that the Super Eagles and Party Jollof rice are the ties that bind Nigerians together; the secret source of our unity. Remove these two elements, and everyone becomes tribal, only favouring their "native soup and tongue". Some learners think that Naija men look at women too much. Queuing for Jollof and eating takes forty minutes. A football match is ninety minutes. No one has looked at a Naija woman for forty minutes before not to talk of a full ninety minutes with extra time added.

Now, we have established that we love to share and stare at food, I would give my own sharing history. I recall sharing everything with my sister. Tough meat had to be divided with the teeth (with eyes shut tight). That was the culture then. Any friend eating anything must share it. It got so bad that even the chewing gum in the mouth was begged for despite protestations from the chewer that "e no sweet again." It didn't improve in University. People shared bottles of Coke and Beer with friends who all put it straight to the mouth.

I mostly ate from my own plate on the dinner table when growing up. There were no gatherings around food sitting on mats. The traditional Nigerian gathering around food has so much to admire. Sitting on a mat on the floor to eat, for one, keeps the hips supple into old age. Just like the village square under the moonlight had everybody out sitting and dancing, the family evening meal brought every one out and stories about the day in the farm could be shared.

Now, I eat alone. I am still the official dust bin for my youngest son. So, if he spits out any food he does not fancy, it is my job to catch and eat it (Too lazy to walk over to the bin).

Sharing a plate with one is manageable in some circumstances. Sharing with two to five people is no problem so long as it is a snack. I, however, don't like to be the one who took the last biscuit. That is usually the one everyone touched. Using the loo in parties is instructive. Hand washing is not a particular priority for some who then bounce out to shake all hands and pick at finger food. And while on the topic, buying food and drinks off street vendors on Lagos roads is like registering for Typhoid Infection. These guys must drink and then urinate during the course of the day and with no public toilets or running water in their "office", one does not need a degree in microbiology from Harvard to understand the threat to health posed by these guys.

Another problem with Crowd Chopping is that start off food quantity is large, and this generates a lot of salivation in the participants. There is zeal to get the work done quickly, so the pace is fast. Experienced Crowd Choppers have cooling facilities in their hands and mouths and have no problem cutting eba at sixty degrees centigrade and tossing it in the hands to cool it off. The pepper soon gets in the nose, and the sneezing starts. Bits of food get repatriated to the plate in a parachute of saliva and sod's law suggests that someone else will eat that food recently exiled from someone else's mouth. There might be add-ons, Hepatitis A, Typhoid, and other various Gastroenteritis, inducing viruses and bacteria in the exiled tiny food portion.

Finger nails can be a problem in communal eating, especially the nail extensions that harbour independent sovereign states of Bacteria. This may sound like *bleachism,* but it would totally freak me out to look into the "yellow Fanta face" of a beautiful co-eater then look down at the pounded yam and see that the same yellow fine girl is the proud owner of a totally dark skinned flaky hand with red long finger nails. I might panic and call the police.

So, in summary, food should have its rightful place as the centre of Naija people's attention, attraction, and affection but while we continue our sharing culture, let it be a one-woman-one-plate arrangement.

OKONKWO

THE CHINESE HAD BEEN IN THE AREA FOR close to six years, building roads and railway lines. Suddenly, news filtered into Ogidi that a laboratory was being moved from Nnewi to the town. An official from the Ministry of Agriculture in Awka had come over to discuss this laboratory with important people in the town. The Chinese had been experimenting with yams for a while now, and Ogidi's soil was considered good for what they intended to do.

The laboratory was ready in two months and was officially opened with much fanfare. The director of the laboratory did not look particularly strong. Mr Wang Li coughed through his speech, and it seemed he might faint under the heat. He spoke of developing yams for export and implored the people of Ogidi that jobs would flow into the area and create prosperity when they started large scale farms. They, however, had to finish all the experiments.

Mr Wang Li surprised everyone when he called for

rotten yams to be brought in for a price. The laboratory was flooded. Mama Nneka, whose kitchen seemed to make yams rot very quickly, made a lot of money when she bought a lot of yams and stored them in her kitchen. She, then, got different people to go in with her rotten yams to collect payment.

This was meant to be for research purposes. It put money in the hands of the people and smiles on their faces. It was announced that, by the next month, land with titles would be bought for farming. The Chinese were paying above the market prices. People queued with their title deeds at the makeshift Land Acquisition porta cabin. A university Professor was worried with the way hectares of land were being sold to foreigners. He asked for a leasing arrangement so that families could continue to have ownership of their ancestral land. He was told to shut up. His father had left him no land to inherit, so who was he to say how land owners should manage their property. He was told, in no uncertain terms, to go and hug his second wife tight and keep his nose out of the business his poverty would not allow him to understand. His books were his second wife.

A particular large land owner refused to sell his land. It was in a prime location and in the area where the Chinese wanted to farm. There were many dignitaries sent to his country house to convince him to put pen to paper and die a billionaire. All his children begged him, but he refused because he had been talking to the professor. He was found dead in bed and the deal went through as his first son was keen on the deal. He had a great befitting burial, and the word around town was that he died of stubbornness.

Mr Wang Li announced that they had grown yams in the laboratory that were resistant to pests and could grow quite large. The community was invited to witness the produce. People came from as far as Obosi, Ihiala, Aguata, and even Onitsha to this big meeting.

The display was impressive. One particular type of yam was huge. In front of it was a plate of cooked slices of yam. Dignitaries who were called up to taste it all nodded as they chewed. This was the best yam ever cooked since the history of the world. The edentulous Mazi Eze was helped onto the podium by his sons. He tasted the yams and clapped his hands in approval. People called the yam *Udoji Award* for its size. Mr Wang Li then went on to announce that this yam could not rot.

Everybody laughed. Mama Nneka, known for her "back luck" kitchen, asked to host the yam for three days, "and una go see".

When two weeks later the *Udoji Award* had not

succumbed to the evil spirits in Mama Nneka's kitchen, people began to take the yam seriously. The murmur in town was that this yam would take over Africa and get Ogidi youth valuable jobs. Things were finally coming together.

A few months to the planting season, the youth of the town were all getting ready for the jobs to come. That was when the shipments began to come in. Lorries delivering mechanical parts arrived to the main farm site which had been cordoned off. Everyone knew the Chinese were building something very great. The town was buzzing with excitement for prosperity had fallen on them uninvited. So many workers came in from China for the construction which went on all day and night. Some youth leaders asked when the locals would start being employed, and they were told that Phase Two of the project would bring the jobs. Soon, people began to hear strange mechanical noises behind the great walls around the farm. No one was allowed in. There was a lot of money in circulation due to the sale of land, so the local economy boomed as people spent lavishly.

An announcement was made that the Yam Farm was going to be officially opened, and a technological miracle was going to be revealed. On the great day, the dignitaries sat in the covered sitting section while the masses stood afar off in the sun. After the speeches and traditional dances, Mr Wang Li announced, "Ladies and Gentlemen, I present to you, Okonkwo!" There was a noise like thunder and out in the distance, what had looked like a heap of sand covered with leaves began to move towards them at great speed. As the leaves flew off to reveal a shiny metallic engine that had a head and eyes, people took to their heels. An announcement was made to calm the crowd, and they slowly returned to watch the spectacle. What followed next was a demonstration of how this machine could prepare the ground, plant seed, spray both water and pesticides, and fell trees. The tree-cutting demonstration was phenomenal. The great machine drove across the large expanse of land and stuck out a giant saw which brought the tree down. This was a robot that would eat Amadioha's lighting as a light snack. It brimmed with the artificial intelligence of an evil spirit.

A man in the crowd shook his head sadly and said, "Farming as an occupation is over in Ogidi." Okonkwo did the entire planting season singlehanded and worked for twenty hours each day. He only stopped to renew his charge from the solar power plant in the corner of the farm. The harvest the next year could have fed the whole of the State.

The produce was displayed for the cameras, and they were promptly shipped off to China. The yam peelings were needed for the development of a Cancer drug that was hoped would fetch the Chinese billions.

Mr Wang Li promised the good people of Ogidi that after the yam peelings have been removed, the rest of the yams would be made into yam powder which the approved importers in Ogidi could buy. He hoped that the government would be able to afford the cancer drugs for the people when it was ready.

People of Ogidi now travelled to Nnewi to buy their yams as they have no farmland to work with. When some young people went to Mr Wang Li to ask for some *Udoji Award* yam seedlings they could plant in other towns, he found it very funny.

"My friends, you don't understand business," he said.

FICTIONAL NDIGBO CHOPPINGS

LONG BEFORE THE ADVENT OF INDOMIE, THE great fictional people that lived in Umuofia to Mbaino (present day South Eastern Nigeria) ate glorious organic food with aromas that could wake up the dead lying in the evil forest. Eating well was a daily occurrence, but come the big feasts such as Weddings or the New Yam festival, no expense was spared in making everyone drunk with alimentary merriment.

No village is complete without the mavericks, and Umuofia had two. One was Nwayieke who loved to pound her foo-foo late at night when mere mortals had eaten and were relaxing in their huts, telling folktales or making babies. She cared nothing for the noise-abatement rules, and her distinctive pestle and mortar broke the silence of the night. The second one was the chief player of them all, Okonkwo who walked like he bounced on springs. He had three wives who had to be satisfied, and that meant eating three meals on some occasions. Their children brought in the dishes fresh off the cooking tripods, and like the equal opportunity husband that he was, he ate all three meals. One could hazard a guess that the wives came to inquire if he had loved the food later in the night personally for some questions are too important to be relayed through one's own children.

This was a village rich in culture and verbosity. You never approached the subject directly but danced around it the way a painful boil is scratched. There was always a preamble, and food was an ever-present metaphor in proverbial sayings. The people said *proverbs are the palm-oil with which words are eaten* after all.

Visitors were welcomed with lavish dollops of proverbs and salutations. Next thing, they broke the Kola to break the ice.

Sensitive things like money and bride price discussions needed to be lubricated with palm wine to keep the Umuofia engine running smoothly.

Okoye called on Unoka (Okonkwo's father) to collect a debt. After pleasantries, Unoka presented *a Kola Nut, some alligator pepper, and a lump of white chalk.*

Okoye accepted the Kola by saying, "*thank you, he who brings Kola brings life.*"

When Okonkwo was starting out in life and needed

a loan of eight hundred seed yams to plant, he turned up at Nwakibie's residence with a pot of palm wine and a cock. Nwakibie, in turn, presents kola nuts and alligator pepper. The kola was broken and prayers said, and those present brought out their drinking horns while Okonkwo shared his palm wine. (Okonkwo drank his wine first — a precaution against poisonous chemicals touching the heart.) They drank palm wine down to the dregs which were handed to Igwelo *who had a job in hand.* He was a newly married man, and palm wine dregs was the Viagra of the time in Umuofia. Following Okonkwo's pitch, the impressed Nwakibie responded thus, "It pleases me to see a young man like you these days when our youth have grown soft." (Chai! Lazy youth?)

Many years later, when Okonkwo had become rich, he was described as having two barns full of yams and three wives. This amount of assets ensured he had his place in Umuofia's Forbes' Rich List because yams were the king of crops, and he had enough to spare. When he was rude to a man who he deemed not to be successful enough to contradict him in a meeting, an elder cautioned him: *those whose palm kernels were cracked for them by benevolent spirits should not forget to be humble.*

A man of great appetite, Okonkwo lost his head

when his wife went to do her hair (Pre Brazilian, perhaps Mbanta extensions) and forgot to make his food. Both angry and hungry, he pounced on her when she returned despite it being the Week of peace when no violence was allowed. Ani, the earth goddess, fined him a she-goat, a hen, a length of cloth, and a hundred cowries. To that, Okonkwo volunteered a pot of palm wine. (The gods too ate regularly.)

The arrival of the feast of the New Yam was an occasion for great joy in celebration of the recent harvest and giving thanks to Ani, the earth goddess. There was feasting all over the town. There was a fable about a man who presented a mountainous amount of foo-foo for guests so much that people on one side did not see those on the other. It was not until evening that guests recognised in-laws over the now-reduced foo-foo and shook hands over it.

The Okonkwo household ate well during the first day of the new yam festival. On the second day, Ekwefi and daughter plucked the feathers of a chicken proving that there might be something to this Black man and chicken stereotype.

Suddenly, the gods sent a blessing that flew in, filling Umuofia with celebration. Locusts descended everywhere, and the elders advised the young ones to wait for nightfall before harvesting the creatures. It was rich picking for Umuofia as dew had soaked up the locust wings, rendering them immobile. The next day, locusts were roasted on clay pots and crunched happily then washed down with palm wine.

After the killing of Ikemefuna, Okonkwo, overcome with grief, did not eat for two days. On the third day, he ate one of his favourite meals — *roasted plantains with slices of oil bean and fish.*

One dark night, Ekwefi and her daughter had delicious *foo-foo and bitter leaf soup.* Then came the folk tale about the greedy tortoise who followed the birds to a great feast in the sky having borrowed feathers from them. As they approached the feast, he was chosen as their spokesman and took on the alias *All of you.* The host presented *pounded yam, yam pottage, a soup full of meat and fish.*

The greedy tortoise asked who the food was for and when the host answered, "*all of you*", he ate most of the food. The angry birds all took their feathers back. The parrot agreed to relay a message to Mrs Tortoise to put out soft furniture so that Tortoise could jump down from the sky. The vindictive bird changed the message and asked for hard objects to be put out. The tortoise jumped down and cracked his shell which had to be put together again by a great medicine man thus losing its smoothness.

Obierika's daughter's *Uri* ceremony saw the whole of Okonkwo's household go in to help with the cooking. They went bearing gifts, and the children made endless trips to the stream. The in-laws were coming to take their bride and brought fifty pots of palm wine for the Umunna.

Cooking pots went up and down the tripods and foo-foo was pounded in a hundred wooden mortars.

Not too long after this great wedding feast, Okonkwo found himself in Mbanta where he spent seven years in exile as punishment for killing a kinsman accidentally when his gun exploded. To thank his in-laws for accommodating him, he threw a generous feast for them before returning home.

Things, however, were not the same anymore. The British had come on iron horses and put a knife to the things that held Umuofia together, and they had fallen apart.

Adapted from the Novel, *Things Fall Apart* by Prof Chinua Achebe

Cows, Herdsmen, and Lovers

The Gangster and his horned love
Spread beef from west to east
They stroll in ancient strides
They are both beauties and both beasts

Born a pretty golden calf
Her leather to the gangster is silk
Now a full grown dame on all fours
She flashes many breasts for sweet milk

Gangster loves his lady's slim tail
Fell in love on an animal farm
As they roam the fine country
They spread jungle laws and evil harm

Moonlight walks singing sweetly
They stop for a bite at the local plantation
Eat up drink up and shoot up the locals
Pack the guns and leave the commotion

Cowboy movies come to life
We enjoyed those bygone Spaghetti Westerns
But what we now have cuts like a knife

Vicious Tuo Shinkafa Northerns

The lady and her gangster
Daily in search of dinner
She wears her ugly perfume
He straps what makes him the killer

They tip the waiters well
Stomach full of bullets, tipped into a grave
The Police all flee the crime scene
The army did not hear so cannot save

Next comes the funeral processions
Black fabrics and swaying leaves
Hallelujah joy we shall meet on that day
Then we pray, all on their knees

Why love what seems to kill us
For after murders by cows and their lovers
The beef has no enemies
We serve beef to all the mourners

Most gangsters guard their wares
With guns that cost much less
But here the case is different
Makes no sense but buy AK 47s nevertheless

The gangster knows you are all addicted
You will buy no matter the human cost

Beef on a pedestal higher than humanity
Shaki, ponmo just buy and ignore the mini holocaust

The gangster is a pimp
He sells his lover at the right price
Then goes to recruit another herd
For meat goes well with Jollof rice

Famine in the land

Echoes and echoes
In the hollow space
A drop of water is heard
Striking the rocks
Emptiness resides where
Once was plenty
I am going to sleep hungry
There is famine in the land

Experts have a revelation
The winds did not herald the clouds
The clouds refused to spit out rain
The earth got dry
And so disgruntled
Would not allow us plant our seed
Tools for harvest
Have a new existence
In the hands
Of men who dig the graves

Mother's plates are clean and dry
Just the way she always wanted
There's no food, so no dirty dishes

Yet somewhere in the world
They have leftovers
She holds me close
And sings a lullaby
Then prays to God
I do not die

The Orphan's song

None has a father
in this orphanage
gone are all hopes of a normal family
even then hope and
redemption will come our way
i believe one day we will be free
Away with hunger
Away with strife
Away away away

Nobody will starve
in this great land of ours
gone are the days of suffering
enough food for all
rice stew and plantain
in our plates are overflowing
Away with hunger
Away with strife

Away away away

GUSTATORY ACCIDENTAL STORIES THAT TOUCH

ANYONE SAT IN THE EATING SEAT HOPES FOR the sweet arrival at the intended destination. That beautiful paradise of satiety. The journey can be beautiful on every turn, especially when eating with someone in love with you or loyal friends who hold you high in regard. Sharing the meal with a Judas leads to tragedies—stories that touch the heart. A simple celebratory meal is converted into a last supper when the guest list is contaminated.

The ones in the driving seats of cars have insurance against accidents, but no one would insure you against gustatory accidents. Those of faith pray before each meal that they don't encounter a mishap while others eat in hope.

There is a legend about eating Naija food that has travelled down the centuries and instils fear in the hearts of the paranoid—the legend of the poisoned plate of food. I have never met anyone who died from

133

intentional food poisoning (never easy to meet dead people), but the rumours are everywhere. Since every Naija who died would have had a last meal, you just don't want to be the one who served the deceased their last meal. The poison-seekers will draw up a nutritional timeline and like a fake Sherlock Holmes, they would point an accusing crooked finger at your kitchen.

Even stranger is the myth of love medicine. The juju is put in the food, the poison makes its way straight to the heart, and the guy falls in love with the girl after eating. Men don't put love medicine in the food of ladies. They just promise the girls thus: "You go chop my money." If only such a juju exists, we can put lorry loads in the River Niger and make all citizens passionately fall in love with the country and not just their pockets!

Naija Food is designed for nutrition, but some chefs just want to give people hypertension by adding so much salt in the pot that you wonder if they misunderstood their pastor who *said, "You are the salt of the earth."*

To the salty insult to the system, some add pepper in a way that induces heartburn guaranteed to keep even people with narcolepsy up all night. It is meant to be pepper added to taste but, in reality, the pepper is added to waste — to waste precious life.

A plate of Naija food is not just for nutrition as lot of therapy is dispensed through the food route, sometimes covertly. A thousand ailments that are presented to "native doctors" are solved by treatments that can be added to food. From stingy husbands to unloving ones, women who consult get oral treatments to introduce into the food with clandestine judiciousness. This is the biggest scam ever as the lady on a mission to medicate will offer the subject's favourite food in the best possible light. To ensure the food is eaten, there would be add-ons like nice clothes and pampering. The recipients eats and naturally would be favourably disposed to the chef. The chef in turn looks for signs of change and takes any unusual blinking of the eyes as proof that the love medicine is working. Both people fall in love, with the guy wondering what has caused a change and the lady convinced the juju has worked.

Bad things happen on the table sometimes, and the most memorable one happened to the Dutch Admiral Baron Jan Gerrit van Wassenaer on the 30th of October, 1723 when he overindulged in food and wine and ruptured his oesophagus. (It was not Jollof rice.) The condition became known as Boerhaave syndrome. Naijaz *say long throat go kill you* with good reason. Eating too much and getting jolly on alcohol and laughter can induce vomiting against a throat that is shut tight in protest. All the pent up pressure in the gullet causes it to burst like a balloon, spilling waves of egusi and native peppers into an evil orbit around the heart.

A funeral usually follows this event for food is all about location. It does well growing on a plant, in the fridge, cooked in a pot or served on a plate. Food does not do well everywhere. In the body, it has to stay in the gullet, stomach and then move along until it exits at the other end. Food outside the long tube that stretches from the mouth to the anus *na die.* If pepper soup and fish go down the wrong path into the lungs, na die. Likewise, if the bowels rupture and their contents spill out into the abdominal cavity, then urgent surgery is required to avoid death.

Outside the body, in the home, for instance, a bowl of egusi poured into a suitcase full of clothes is a disaster.

Stretching the stomach to the limit and then topping it with alcohol is practically having one foot in the grave. *Come and quench syndrome.* Little stones in beans that crack the teeth, food allergies enlarging the tongue, and choking on one's food when eating and laughing at the same time all range from the irritating to the fatal in terms of adverse gustatory experiences.

That typhoid infection makes the skin crawl. You eat a meal, lick your fingers, and think it is all over, but it isn't. The bacteria rot the intestines, and the eater soon realises that the journey of thousand miles to the grave starts with a swallow. But the worse of all is cholera. There might have been no good meal to indulge in save drinking a glass of contaminated water. Soon, floodgates open at both ends and, torrential fluids splash out like it is Victoria Falls in the rainy season. Cholera never looks good in Naija obituaries, so the victim is announced to the world as having succumbed to a brief illness.

As far as irritating things go, worm infestations top the list. I once had a patient vomiting worms through the mouth and nose, with one wiggling worm stuck in the nostril. Now how is that for a return on investment? Eating stew with a few eggs of worms and having a nation of parasites living in the gut and sucking the life out of a human being. When evil parasites want a place to live in, they don't go to an estate agent and pay a deposit like everyone else and subsequently sign a tenancy agreement with the proposed landlord. They come in via 419 (deception), swimming in food that is loved, staying naked to the eye. No one would eat a plate of rice garnished with wriggling worms, and so the parasite hides as tiny eggs in the meat which retains its taste. A delicious meal washed down with sweet drinks while the nice music plays becomes part of the narrative on a hospital bed — a gustatory story that touches the hearts of the hearers but kills the protagonists.

All Naijaz have an eating disorder: binge eating at parties. Watch carefully at your next Naija party. People can be caught eating food weighing more than their youngest child. Anorexia and Bulimia are non-existent in Naija as those are usually diseases of prosperous nations. Naijaz are in survival mode, so the mindset is that of a permanent *eat-all-you-can-eat buffet* for who knows tomorrow. *Dat sef na gustatory narrative that touches.*

SOMETHING LIGHT

Unscrupulous individuals give *something light* a bad name. You know them. They consider eating two portions of pounded yam, each the size of a new born baby's head as something light. Simply because they usually eat eight portions but are now down with malaria and have lost the inbuilt greed. *The greedy ones have all been born.*

We are here to claim *light* back from the darkness of crude greed. The *light something* is really a snack. It is a portion of food that will not stretch the belly of a toddler. This is food that caresses the palate and makes the mouth yearn for more. Pepper soup, thin slices of pawpaw, akara, few ground nuts and the like.

I must warn that when a Naija uses the word *something* in reference to food, they are lying at worst or being vague and misleading at best. Like the guy who is invited to join someone eating a meal who says, "Thanks, I have just had *something.*" The fact that he strokes his abdomen as he speaks and looks at the plate with lust betrays his hunger. Naijaz can be vague when it comes to food and might even give unwanted details. Offer some people a drink and they tell you how full they are by not only listing the meals they have had in the last twenty hours, but they throw in the genealogy of the goat that featured in the pepper soup. Then they drink three bottles because "you insisted."

Snacks which are also called small chops are the real light *somethings*. Naijaz have incorporated foods from all over the world in the creation of our small chops list, but I will concern myself with snacks which can best be described as authentic Naija food.

There is no place like a Naija wedding to understand the importance of small chops. The affairs tend to run late because of circumstances beyond anyone's control, and it seems the late arrival of key participants is always linked to a hair dresser. So you leave the church and take photographs, then it is off to the wedding reception. With everyone hungry, people are ushered to various tables. Like it is in FIFA World Cup Groups, there is always that Group of death. The table that devours its inhabitants because there is a super hungry guy with a prominent Adam's apple sitting there. The type of guy Fela sang about in the song Kalakuta show:

Look di man he dey waka
Hunger dey run for im face (woko woko woko woko)

Once seated at this table, the lateness continues, and the DJ tries his best to help you forget your hunger by making you deaf. Then the small chop bowls arrive, Hallelujah! Then, malt drinks with no bottle top openers. Now due to politeness, no one wants to be the first to make a move for the snacks, and a gentleman will usually offer the bowls of finger foods to the ladies. But not on the table of death and starvation. The super hungry man just reaches out with hands as big as shovels and grabs all the puff puff. Next, he brings out his bottle opener from his bunch of twenty keys (which includes a miniature pen knife), and opens two bottles of malt for himself! At this stage, the wise people excuse themselves and seek another table.

The small chops are used to keep you hanging on while you endure stale jokes from the MC that you have read on your WhatsApp groups years ago. That is until the main food arrives — party jollof rice.

Here is a list of the life-saving snacks that keep Naijaz from fainting at weddings and parties operating on African time.

Puff puff

Small, tasty and just like Bonny Light, easily

processed, this snack is the King of all Naija finger foods. Couples that had no puff puff at their wedding reception need to go and remarry themselves. It is made from frying a mixture of plain wheat flour, oil, and dried yeast until it becomes golden brown.

Chin chin

This crunchy snack that comes in small hard cubes is prepared from deep frying dough made up of plain flour and margarine. This snack should come with a health warning. The hard granite like cubes of goodness can break a tooth or dislocate a jaw bone. All dignity is lost as the jaws are converted into a pressurised grinding machine, causing the chin to vibrate at an astounding frequency. Maybe this chin action gives the snack its name.

While on the topic of losing dignity, we might as well go there.

Sugar cane

I call this the snack of madness. A country eats all its sugar cane and imports sugar? It is messy to eat and spit out. People look like Pandas eating bamboo when they feast on sugar cane. It is child abuse to have kids clear up the mess after adults have eaten this snack. The worse comes when the sugar ants congregate on the messy leftovers. Thank goodness, no one has been mad enough to serve this Bamboo lookalike at a wedding ceremony.

Nuts

Groundnuts and guguru (popcorn) keep the mouth busy and keep hope alive while waiting for the Party Jollof rice. The only problem here is people dip their fingers in the nuts, and some fall back into the bowl. Now, I have been to parties and seen how some people wash their hands in the loo. Enough said.

Akara

Bean cakes are Naija's equivalent to hot crossed buns. They have the powers to ginger you out of your lethargic state on a cold harmattan morning especially when there is ogi (pap) to assist it in the journey down that dark tunnel that leads to the stomach. It is made from frying blended beans which has been spiced to taste.

Plantain Trilogy

Thin fried slices of unripe plantain are called ipekere (plantain chips) and when ripe plantain is fried, it is called dodo. Roast plantain is boli. Dodo goes well with rice, yam, and moin-moin.

Meats

Snails, gizzards, suya, and kilishi (dried beef) can be used as starters before the main meal.

Miscellaneous

Other snacks which are usually not available in weddings but can be obtained from road side food vendors include, suya, roasted or boiled maize alongside coconut, fried yams and various fruits such as oranges, agbalumo, banana, mangoes, and pears.

Kuli kuli, which is fried peanut paste, is popular for some just like coconut candy. Some snack on tapioca and other love termites and maggots off the palm trees. Mosa, which is fried mash plantain mixed with eggs, pepper, and flour is eaten in Northern Nigeria.

Summary

For some, anything that is not *swallow* (foods swallowed whole without the need for chewing such as foo foo and pounded yam) is something light. People like this never waste time with snacks. The party starts for them when the swallow arrives. We hope and pray that something light will appear at the end of their dark tunnel of consumption one day.

THAT'S THE WAY THE RICE GOES

THAT PHRASE, *"POINT AND KILL"*, SAYS IT ALL. the death of a plant or animal comes before a meal. Next the preparation, the cooking, and finally the eating happens. A lot of activity goes on before the spoon arrives at the opening of the mouth. Just as people vary in social status, so does the pre-mastication routine. Even the plates and utensils for eating come in grades. But once that spoon goes between the teeth, the digestion process shows itself to be fully democratised; that is just the way rice goes.

It is the same process for all once that alimentary mechanism kicks in.

For the uninitiated, *point and kill* refers to the makeshift aquarium usually situated in the corner of an eating house where the customers drift to and choose the fish they want by pointing that index finger of death. The fish is then prepared and served up for the paying guest. It does not come fresher than this.

The jollof rice, moin-moin and fresh fish are on a

continuous journey called *the journey of life*. It is a shame that many Naijaz have sat before plates for decades and still don't know what happens to the jollof once they have buried it in their mouths. Hopefully, this article will shed some light.

For starters, the teeth are not just for smiling on Instagram upandan. Biting, chewing, and the production of saliva all happen in the mouth. This converts food of various sizes and textures into a bolus that can finally be swallowed down the oesophagus (gullet).

The back of the throat is such a wonderful place — a point of no return. There lies the junction where the road forks into two with one going down the wind pipe for breathing and the other one going straight to the stomach. Let's just say that the wind pipe leading to the lungs has a two-way traffic rule but transmits just air while the gullet is a one-way-one-lane express way (shayo masters might disagree). The gullet admits numerous things, but just one grain of rice down the wind pipe leads to choking. Naijaz may disobey traffic laws, but they would never drive their pounded yams down the wind pipe. (Na who wan die?)

Before the spoon actually gets to the mouth, the cooking process produces aromas that stimulate salivation. By the time the spoon arrives, the lubrication for swallowing is abundantly present.

It's the fish on the flame
Can't you smell the aroma?
That's the point and the kill
I'm drowning in saliva

Saliva is not just water however. It contains salivary amylase which breaks down some of the starch in food, hence the observation of people who chew long enough start to experience — the food gets sweeter the more they chew. Unfortunately, these are the ones who chew forever and still insist on arguing over Naija politics with food in their mouth. (Nothing is uglier than masticated food in the mouth of anyone save your own children).

Once into the stomach, that great big washing machine churns everything around for hours. A plate of food usually consists of carbohydrates (jollof), protein (fish), fat (oil) vitamins and mineral salts. Depending on which African films are watched, you might want to add love potions or poisons to this list. While the mineral salts and vitamins need no digestion, everything else gets broken down. This breakdown process is not different from Nigeria's crude oil being broken down to petrol, diesel, kerosene, petroleum jelly, and many other wonderful substances able to make people rich.

The stomach produces acid and pepsin which breaks down protein. As the churned food moves into the duodenum, a message is sent to the gall bladder which contracts and sends in the bile required to emulsify the fat (which was added to the jollof). That same message gets to the pancreas that lies behind the stomach, and it sends its own contribution to the chemical reaction namely trypsinogen for the breakdown of protein (fish), lipase for the breakdown of oil aided by the bile salts and pancreatic amylase for the carbohydrate (jollof). As the food is transported along the small intestine, it gets mixed well with the enzymes to ensure the chemical reaction continues. The end products of digestion begin to get absorbed through the gut wall.

The gut is one long tube or perhaps one long bus route in Lagos. The conductor announces the various bus stops and no passenger leaves. Only enzymes (chemical passengers) enter and start to ruffle up the exiting passengers all the way to the final bus stop. It is here the conductor shouts, "Toilet!" And everybody shouts, "Owa!"

The small intestine is a long journey of winding narrow roads without street lights. The further along the journey, the more area boys begin to show up (bacteria), and they are not without their usefulness.

Soon, the food becomes completely unrecognisable as it approaches that junction that marks the beginnings of the large bowel — the ileocaecal valve. From here onwards, the water is sucked right out of the food which can now be called stool. Traffic is slow for maximum extraction of every last drop of moisture from the stool. Like cars stuck in traffic, the life is slowly drained out of the passengers, and that strong smell of fumes become suffocating.

Round the bends they drive until it all comes to the great hold up at the rectum. The horns blare loudly, singing with a tone that cannot be ignored: "Give me a chance. I want to come through." This call of nature is usually obeyed promptly.

So, what is the point of all the drama with *point and kill* fish, jollof rice, moin-moin, and dodo? Why should there be a long food preparation process? Why can't we just have taps that flow with protein shakes, carbohydrate fluids, and fat juices? The acquisition of raw food materials followed by cooking in a hot kitchen seems like too much work.

Personally, if given the choice between a drink of tasteless amino acids or a chicken roasting in the oven and filling the house with the aroma that gives the stomach hope of good things coming, I will choose the latter. The sitting around the table and going through the act of eating is a great social event. Most great partnerships usually start with that first tentative meal together. Breaking bread, breaking ice and then feeling your way through is how business is done. The journey is just as exciting as arriving at the destination.

Life is about the process. Breaking complex things down and then reassembling them up again. Ultimately, the body works on fuel, and it is nice that this fuel comes into our fuel tanks through pleasurable means unlike those poor cars at petrol stations that get lifeless fuel pumps stuck into them while they stand looking totally bored.

THE SMELLY COLONY

THE SUPERMODEL BLESSED WITH A BEAUTIFUL face and perfect torso looks flawless on the runway. Movements on the runway stir the emotions and distract from a dark secret. For, in there, somewhere in the centre of her beautiful being, is a long dark pipe called the small intestine and colon. Never seen by her but the effects are what we all see. She sees the beautiful dividends of colonic action only in the mirror. Enzymes cursed with anonymity and enslaved to a life time of digestion without pay or pension, working hard on raw materials to produce life sustaining goodness.

Few human beings on earth have ever beheld their colons, and when they do, they usually do not live to tell the tale. The same appears to the case with the really powerful seats of power that have reigned through the ages. Kings and Queens usually never visit the colonies but wax great on what the colonies produce.

When Peter came into the house, Jesus was the first to speak. "What do you think, Simon?" he asked. "From whom do the kings of the earth collect duty and taxes — from their own children or from others?"

"From others," Peter answered.

Subjects that are lucky enough to live close to the palace behold the splendour bestowed on princes and princesses who live off the proceeds of colonial taxes and benefits, yet out of sight is out of mind. The people never know much about the sweat and blood which goes on in the colonies. Like freshly baked loaves, the royals of old had an attractive smell that attracts. It is that sweet smell of success that the people love to be around. It is such a beautiful cloud of perfume that rains blessings on the soul. Smells also warn people to flee the scatological entities in the colon. Like petrifying corpses, the smell goes ahead of them to warn people to move in opposite directions.

Just like beautiful people never see their intestines, colonial powers never explain the inner workings of the empire to the sons of the soil. This makes the citizens begin to believe their birth right is to possess a heightened sense of entitlement and to enjoy the best that the planet has to offer and that things will always work out this way as if by magic.

Mesenteric veins take the goodness from the intestines back to be used by the human body to run its economy (or perhaps its physiology). There has to be ready channels to repatriate value back to the seat of power after all. No matter how long and tortuous the intestines are, sometimes looking like tubes that could stretch around the world, there is always a vein sending nutrients back. All prosperous economies since the world began grew fat on the backs of tribute or income from the colonies. Every stage has a backstage and every well-stocked shopping mall is connected to a dark sweat shop in a dark smelly corner of the planet. The world is now a global village, and the goodness continues to flow from the dark places to the well-lit places.

Men go miles into the ground daring to trend in places that kill both man and birds with noxious gasses. They come up from the darkness of the mines with diamonds and then retire for the night in poor housing. The end consumer is beautiful and gets to wear a ring gifted to her by her lover. Despite the professional interest of miners, nobody says that a diamond is a miner's best friend. The miners work like slaves and risk their lives to put food on the table, an activity with little scope for job satisfaction, while the beautiful girl is happy to receive that "rock". She is not likely to see a miner all her life or even visit a mine shaft the exact same way that she is unlikely to ever see her own colon.

Some people and various anatomical organs on the planet are here to work and never be seen. Some people on the planet are in the know. They have inside information, and they see everything. Most are oblivious to many things. The surgeon might handle the colon daily, but there is no chance of daily pictures on social media. Very little information is for sharing. In colonial times and even in the days of slavery, the top people who owned shares in the big trading companies knew where their bread was buttered, but they never went into graphic detail too often.

The people in England's cotton mills enjoyed the massive employment than cotton brought with little thought for where the cotton was grown and under what conditions the human labourers lived. The anus is not too far from the colon, and it is no wonder that former colonies end up with the stench of the products the anal department are well known for, leading to the latrine-countries' phenomenon.

Nigeria was once dotted with empires that had powerful thrones and collected tributes from conquered neighbours who provided human capital for the slave trade. The Kanem-Bornu, in the North east, the Oyo Empire in the South West, and the Benin

Empire in the south central regions all had booming economies and their own colonies at various times in history.

The Portuguese arrived in the Benin Empire in 1485 and found an organised nation. Better naval skills and fire power meant that all the peoples and empires were rounded up under one giant umbrella — Nigeria, the colony of Great Britain (put up or get shot). Today's empire could be tomorrow's colony or latrine country. Rise and fall, the circle keeps on going. What goes around comes around as happens in planetary rotations.

The Benin of 1485 was an independent state that could survive without any foreign help. Today's Benin City in Edo state is far from independent. Beyond the global village and its co-dependencies, the basics that are needed for modern life: cars, planes, computers and most equipment needing steel, are all imported. It does not take much thinking to conclude that dependent states will become poor, and poverty stinks even more that the insides of a colon that has lost its blood supply. Some citizens have suffered so much hardships and gangrenous poverty to the point where they have cried out in anguish: *"life in Nigeria was better when the country was a colony."*

A survey of brides wearing diamond wedding

rings will reveal few have a clue about mines and the Dutch brothers, Diederik and Johannes De Beer, who found diamonds on their farm and sold the farm for £6, 600. The company which later bore their name — De Beers — has since made billions (a bit like the MacDonald's Brothers' story). Without specific education, it is hard to know these things.

A survey of the average Joe Blogs walking the streets of London will reveal that knowledge about how England has benefitted from Africa is scanty or non-existent. The common knowledge is that Africa generates immigrants and nothing else. Without specific education, it is hard for English people to know how lucrative the African branch of the British Empire has always been.

A survey of super models walking the streets of London will reveal that knowledge about how their beautiful bodies have benefitted from their colons is scanty or non-existent. The common knowledge is that colons and intestines generate farts, stools, and nothing else. Without specific education, it is hard for people to know how lucrative the colonic department of the body has always been.

THE HARDEST NAIJA MEALS TO MAKE

COOKING IS LIKE BRINGING LOVE AND beauty to the world. The chef has ingredients playing their individual instruments in a gastronomic orchestra which has to be blended seamlessly into a homogenous entity. The audience come for love and beauty. Once that curtain is drawn and the burners come on, the clock starts ticking and the already great expectations go through the roof. It is a big responsibility to satisfy the hungry with love and beauty served on a plate. Each comes with an appetite and some sense of entitlement. They might have paid some money or perhaps feel that family ties qualify them to be fed on demand.

Just like the great orchestra conductor's work does not start at show time, the same applies to the chef. There are manuscripts to pore over, ancient recipes for success that have to be practiced over and over again. Instruments have to be in tune and played with fervour. The chef plans the meal, keeps a mental note of what elements are needed, and goes to great trouble to assemble a great cast. Once the burners come on, it is a race against the clock. The meat would not be fresh forever and once in the hot water, it has a narrow window of opportunity to transform from raw talent to finished article while at the same time being in rhythm with every other pot occupant that gets added at different stages of the performance. Movements of the hand come at strategic times in the process, and the chef conducts alone.

The Urhobos have a soup called *esha* (*isha*) cooked with a special *esha* beans that needs six hours of cooking as a preliminary before the soup is cooked the next day. The most popular Urhobo soup is *owoevwri* (*owo soup*) which can be ready in ninety minutes. If owo is a 100-metre sprint, then *esha* is an arduous marathon. Esha, no doubt, is the hardest soup to make in Urhobo land (located in the Niger Delta) and was only eaten in my childhood at the Christmas and New Year seasons when there was time to prepare the ingredients and boil the beans that took forever to get cooked.

The preparation of akpu from the cassava stage is another lengthy process. There are some meal preparations that can best be described as aerobic workouts or hard labour. Long before the arrival of instant pounded yam powders (that contain rice, potatoes, and starch with about only 60-70% yam) l, people actually pounded boiled yam in a mortar with a pestle. As a young lad, it was not unusual to hear Lagos neighbours pounding away across the street. In a tropical country, sweat flies everywhere at the hint of exertion, and this was why we always heard the wives talk about *all the sweat I have put into this marriage* during every marital dispute.

The Naija kitchen can be a very hot and lonely place. It is predominantly inhabited by the ladies (or female domestic home helps). Some things make the meals very hard to conjure up and in retrospect, it has nothing to do with the technicalities of the food-making process. Below are a list of the hardest Naija meals to make.

- **Cooking meals with limited money**

Once the next meal's arrival is unsure, the meal at hand becomes hard to make. Positive people may say, "Eat today and sleep but let tomorrow take care of tomorrow." One really needs a strong mind, bursting with faith to cook the last food in the house, singing happily and knowing full well that hunger like mosquitoes always come back. Mum may not announce to the family that she is serving the last supper to spare the kids of the burden of worry. Some kids might complain about what's for supper during the cooking process. That is when sweat and tears mix on a sad face.

I don't know where the next meal is coming from.

• Cooking for funerals

At a time when the bereaved should be comforted, they are busy cooking for the whole village in the name of doing a befitting burial. Men in black turn up looking a bit sad then give the bereaved a hug worth N1000 and proceed to drink beer and wine worth N3, 000 and eat food worth N6, 000. Why should someone who has just had the worst news of their lives be at the market buying dry fish and yams by the truck load? The ironic thing is if the food is very good, greedy relatives would start to ask if there was a will and if their name was mentioned in it. Cooking under these circumstances is tiring. People would gladly cook four times the amount of food and go days without sleep for a joyful occasion such as a wedding, but Naija culture wants a carnival because someone had a stroke and died.

• Cooking for a neurotic man

Some Naija men don't eat soups that have been in

the fridge. It has to be straight from the pot to the plate. This kind of men are not usually the indomie type. It has to be pounded yam and their favourite soup. You wonder what these men think refrigeration was invented for. Talk about a hard knock life!

These crazy men also never cook. It is almost as absurd as a guy saying he never watches highlights of his team's Premiership matches on the television as his taste is live games. Then he asks someone else to buy his season ticket for home games and pay his transport costs and stadium entry fees for all away matches. My village people will tell him that before you grow the teeth of a rabbit, be prepared to grow the lip to cover it. New soup ko, new flame ni.

- **Cooking when pregnant**

To bend down and open the oven can be problematic when you are carrying a large oven in your abdomen.

- **Cooking while lonely and depressed**

The monotony of doing repetitive tasks that have been done so many times before such as peeling potatoes or slicing tomatoes means that one slips into automatic actions needing no thoughts as all actions are done instinctively. That is when the mind really travels. Regrets, sadness, guilt, people who are missed all come flooding into the mind. Tears flow while standing alone in a hot kitchen. No one but the chef knows how hard it was to get those plates of food infused with love and beauty to the table.

CHRISTMAS FOOD

IN MY CHILDHOOD YEARS, CHRISTMAS DID not come quietly, not in the middle of an oil boom. There were trips to the tailors for Christmas clothes. Shoes were bought, tried and then locked away because "they are for Christmas."

Items of food and drink began to show up which we gazed at like that twinkling star which lead wise men to Bethlehem. Cartons of Star larger were stacked in the corner surrounded by crates of Coca Cola and Fanta. These were rows of bottles in wooden crates standing in corners. No one went too close because they were for Christmas. We harboured wicked thoughts in our young minds about what we were going to do to those drinks. In the crates, a missing bottle was obvious but come Christmas, when the migration to the fridge starts, nobody would keep records of coke bottles census figures, and the drinking frenzy goes into overdrive.

Great expectations gripped Lagos as white

envelopes flooded the letter boxes (well, we didn't have a letter box. The post man put the letters between coils of cables at the electric metre), and once opened, the cards were arranged on a string that went from one end of the room to the other.

With time, another string was needed, and we ended up with a giant X on the ceiling. Once in a while, someone forgot and switched on the ceiling fan, and the cards hit the ceiling. We just couldn't wait for Christmas. That was the day you wore new clothes right down to underwear and socks. Complete with a plastic sun glasses, and the swag was on fire.

The obligatory trip to Kingsway Stores to see Father Christmas brought us plastic pistols helping to distract from the wait for the big day. Money soon began to flood the pocket as adults grew generous as if the harmattan air had brought some *goodwill to all men* with it.

We had chewing gums, goody-goody, trebor refreshers, and tom-tom all day long. It was a joyful feasting season in December. There was spare change for night action: fireworks. Every night, it went *bang, bang, bang* as mini explosions lit the night up. Rockets flew up and exploded into numerous diamonds, and there was always the smell of festive stew in the air.

When the school finally closed for the merry

holidays, a good report card secured extra rewards. One played and ate all day.

The visitors soon began to arrive and like it was the custom in the seventies, you entertained them. White Horse Whisky, Cartons of Star larger and crates of "minerals" were how people entertained. Music blared from the gramophone (O come all ye faithful), and a visit could soon turn into a party. King Sunny Ade and the Chief Commander Ebenezer who must be *Obeyed* had a musical rivalry that usually played out the fiercest at the Christmas (Keresimesi) season. With few people owning phones, you never knew who was coming, and it was not usual to have three families arrive unannounced. The Christmas decorations were now up. No Christmas tree showed up in our house, but there were glittering bits all over the place. We had colourful paper Bells that opened up, bright red pictures of a white Santa and many images of animals in the snow (a bit confusing for us as there was no snow in Lagos).

Rice and stew very plenty was the norm. Christmas rice was enchanting and the dodo divine. The moin-moin came in its original leaves and one unpeeled the botanical package with anticipation. Once delivered, the moin-moin was incised through the centre to find out if Father Christmas had ordained boiled egg or corned beef in the centre. That one-child-one-piece-of-meat ordinance was thrown out of the window. The only limitation to our eating was the size of our stomachs.

Some family friends had a carol service for the children, and we all went there to sing and then eat. The party jollof rice made us undergo growth spurts. The street hawkers did brisk business. Those were the days a driver called an orange seller, and she puts down her tray and gave a performance of dexterity in peeling the fruit. The question at the end of the task always amazed me.

"How make I cut am?"

The options were to slice it across its equator or to carve out a cone at the North Pole. As one of the equatorial disposition, I never could understand those who choose a North Pole cone as it meant they had to squeeze out the juice in the South Pole right past the equator northwards to the open cone up north.

The kids gathered around the driver (on minimum wage) with begging eyes, and the spirit of Christmas pulls at his heart strings and manipulates him into buying oranges for us all. With older siblings on holiday, there were more people to pester when the ice cream van came along. Any hawker got called. Mangoes, coconut, corn, pawpaw, agbalumo, and the guguru and epa sellers who also put up a show, throwing groundnuts in the air and blowing away its skin.

Soon the bleating of goats and rams could be heard in the mornings as Christmas day loomed. The chicken population in the neighbourhood rose astronomically. Like wicked Herod killed all the babies at the first Christmas, Lagosians slaughtered all the animals on Christmas Eve.

Honourable mention must be made of one jollof rice I ate at new Estate Baptist church in the run up to one Christmas. It was a carol service followed by Christmas cheer. I believe I am what I am today because of the jollof, dodo, and moin-moin that tasted like Angel Gabriel had flown by with some heavenly maggi sauce to sprinkle over the pot (see me salivating here o!). It was truly a case of:

Joy to the world, the Lord has come.

Bottled drinks in crates had an aura in my childhood. You knew they were coming because they rattled, and like the dogs in Pavlov's experiments, we salivated and lost concentration on item six as item seven on the programme was imminent.

You swallowed spit as you sang — O little town of Bethlehem — for that jollof smell travels faster than the speed of light. You feel it in your soul. It you came first that first term of school, you told everyone for you did not know who will "dash you Christmas money."

Those were heady times when you visited people with full stomachs and still had the intestinal fortitude to squeeze in more food.

The stars of December with jollof rice, moin-moin, all Nigerian soups, stew, all meat and fish, more stew, ukodo and eshia with dry fish and freshly boiled yams. And to have all these dishes being cooked simultaneously was one of the joys of being alive then. The frying of meat was also good as you could take a piece from the already prepared heap without anyone noticing. Like all families, we had tales of Christmas time that have been told and re-told through the years.

Like the time when mum brought home a frozen turkey as hand luggage from London as she was landing back in Lagos on Christmas Eve. But the biggest story was that of the turkey my father brought home that became part of the family. It knew us and played with us when we fed it. It was a tragic day when it faced execution on that Christmas Eve. Just like Ikemefuna cried to Okonkwo that faithful night when things fell apart, so did our turkey. "My Father, my father," it screamed, looking at the family conjuring up further images of a fearful young Elisha crying as Elijah ascended to heaven. The last words the Turkey heard before the brutal beheading was "Father, for what? In this Lagos?"

I was moved to my soul and lowered my young head in quiet prayer. "May your flesh rest in peace on my plate of jollof rice come Christmas day."

Hallelujah! My prayers were answered.

Daughter's cooking

My lovely daughter's cooking
Is exactly just like mine
We know that dinner's ready
From the noisy smoke alarms
Some homes ask, "What is for dinner?"
Some say, "What's smelling nice?"
I walk in through the doors
And ask, "What's smelling burnt for supper?"
The Christian upbringing?

She serves up burnt offerings
Or dad's a doctor?
She loves killing all bacteria
There is no risk of Salmonella
Sometimes, no risk of food
And when she puts her mind to it
She incinerates all veg and meat

I pray she marries well
Maybe a strong fireman
Or even a rich footballer
With chefs in every kitchen

But then, she just might learn
To turn down all that heat
And that will be the very day
The pigs learn how to fly

Eating Books

Sugary puff puff fertilised my joy
On the sunny fields of infant life
Sprinkled from tree tops with yellow showers
I read the food and ate the books

Lava set on a slopping hill side
Was how my beans looked congealed in Finbarrs
Studded with rocks of dodo and streams of stew
The rare meaty gem thrown in
In the dinning arena of Akoka

Tuwo shinkafa in muddy okra
Followed the snacks of meat pies and caprisone
Food flowed like a River in Kaduna
Sweet long two hours was guava time
Rewards for trespassing the angry farmers plot
His arrow missed our heads
We didn't go back to read the fruits between meals of
books

The MamaPuts of Ugbowo campus
In Benin stood like pyramids
Certificates and diplomas

Now hang in offices
Tasty memories hang in our hearts
Of when men were boys
When we read plates during breaks from meals of
books

Mama Pharaoh

On this Campus none more important
Like the Madam who feeds us all
For though the theories sound brilliant
Can't satisfy when man must wack

I am here for major academics
And eba-ogbono lingual gymnastics
If I ever gra-du-ate
Post me soups in familiar plastics

After Youth Service comes employment
House, car and then I will marry
Just one key to my contentment
Babe must cook like Mama Pharaoh

MAMAPUT AND PAPATAKE

IT IS JUST LIKE WALKING AROUND TOWN WITH two fridges on the chest. Nursing mothers multi-task doing both the production and storage of the milk behind closed brassieres while still being on stand-by to feed the hungry at the hint of a cry. Sonny Okosun in his politically charged song *Papa's Land* asked, *we wanna know who owns the land, Papa's land*. He was agitating against the Apartheid system that had Black Sons of the soil in South Africa receive second-class status despite being original inhabitants of the African land. It was this patch of soil he referred to as Papa's Land. It was true that the Papas grabbed plots here and there, but when hunger strikes, it is Mama Africa that feeds the continent.

Women worldwide serve more plates to the hungry than men. In Nigeria, the men eat more than they cook except for *ssuya* and *mai shai* (breakfast buka) which are always managed by men. Women preparing and selling suya by the road side is as rare as a buka where the cooking is done predominantly by men. I wouldn't eat in any of these kind of rare establishments if I happened to come across them for I would be too busy fainting.

Men grab most of the lucrative television chef contracts and star in the statehhouses, ppalaces, and top restaurants of the world, but the MamaPuts feed the nations in all the continents. While Nigerians call MamaPut the local low-cost restaurants that feed the masses, today I define MamaPut as all the women who put food into the hungry mouths of the world.

I have long forgotten most of the people I met while in University, but I still recall the local MamaPut who I have renamed Mama Pharaoh. I wrote about her in the draft of my novel *Blind Procedure* (which is still being written since 2005).

MAMA PHARAOH

On this campus none important
Like the madam who feeds us all
For though the theories sound so brilliant
Can't satisfy when man must wack

IT LOOKS LIKE MAMA AFRICA GAVE THE continent every chance of prospering. The fertile soil and abundant fresh water supply means seeds thrown out of the window just grow. In addition, there are women everywhere even more fertile than the soil. It is almost like some ladies get pregnant if their man looks at them longer than two minutes straight. These ladies are ever ready to put food in the mouths of Africans, but they lack power to ensure that food production is adequate. Many women are involved in African agriculture, but the policy makers tend to be dominated by the Papas. The land ownership, fertilisers, and pesticides are in male control, and mismanagement is a major problem. The Papas love to dip their hands in the till. The poverty that makes people have no funds to buy food is imposed on Africa by the Papas who do not make the right moves to grow the economy. The MamaPuts have their hands handcuffed behind their backs, yet they are the ones that can feed Africa.

An ever-so-kind Mama Africa studded the soil with gold, diamonds, and natural gas. These were solely to feed the people. The Papas had other plans. They flare the gas in Nigeria while MamaPuts struggle cooking with fire wood. They mined and they took the diamonds, along with their foreign partners. In some areas, Mama Africa was stabbed through the belly until she bled crude oil to be shipped out to foreign refineries. The cash generated stays in the hands of the Papas who take.

The land-grabbing and cash-grabbing are ironic habits. No matter how much is accumulated, everyone dies and leaves it behind. The poor ones who starve despite the potential to produce ample amounts of food die. The frustrated MamaPuts who could not fulfil their purpose in full also die knowing they could have put more food in hungry mouths. The greedy Papas die and all they get is gold-plated coffins and a befitting burial, and the food they refused to give Africans in life is eaten off their bodies by the African earth worms six feet under (DJ play some Astronomia here).

When simple things are not done, Warri go say, *"no be ordinary eye."* Ordinary eyes would see the obvious and take action according to what is seen. Blind eyes, on the other hand, look at things but are unable to make simple conclusions.

It is a curse for someone in a position of power to embezzle money that could be used to ensure good harvest yields and lower food prices. The blindness looks even more bizarre when the white-collared crook buys a limousine and drives through town, and the very starving people who he has defrauded sing his praises. The same applies to electricity which has everything to do with the availability of food for the MamaPuts. Many times, African countries cannot store farm produce for lack of refrigeration. AC currents were invented by Nikola Tesla in 1888, and before that, refrigerator that used vapours to lower temperatures was invented in 1805 by Oliver Evans. One would have thought that by now every farm, factory, and house in Africa would have electricity and contain fridges for food storage. That is still not the case.

There is a short-term gain in stealing the money that fuels development. The Papas buy flash clothes and houses shining like a solitary torchlight in the heart of darkness. It is a bit like taking a pistol and shooting all competitors at the start of a race on the right foot and then racing on to victory. Only psychopaths enjoy that kind of victory which comes at the great expense of others. Welcome to the crazy world of African leaders (PapaTakes) who wrestle out starvation from the jaws of abundance.

THE FAECAL RESIDENTS

WE ARE ALL FULL OF FAECAL RESIDENTS; that is if we choose to believe what our distractors tell us. Perhaps there is a little truth here. Occupied intestines lie deep inside everyone. We take our guts to parties, work, and out running. Some go so far as calling their deep premonitions *gut feelings*. Hidden under skin and designer clothes, these organs of chemical reactions stay hidden from the outside world primed for war. Eating is war, but it does not always seem so.

All warfare is deceptive is a saying hued out of the pages of *The Art of War* by Sun Tzu. The food on a plate in a fine restaurant knows not what is in store as it sees itself transported on a spoon past lips coated with lipstick and then past a row of beautifully set white teeth. As soon as the first bite hits, the food soon knows that the mouth that kisses also has a killer bite.

The intestines are one smelly slimy place, but the good news is that it is a smell-proof chamber and impervious to *death-carrying* bacteria ready to take out their landlord at the first chance.

People talk about all the haters out there plotting mischief while they omit to realise that the real haters lie within them. They say that an ocean faring vessel is not threatened by the depth of the surrounding waters but by the waters that may get into it. The enemy within is most lethal. We all practically walk around with non-ticking bombs inside no matter how beautiful our bodies look. Our guts can teach us a lot about life. It is our own internal workings that slow us down. Not some imaginary foes out there. We have a war in our minds, and the number one enemy to personal progress does not lie in a faraway politician's house but in our hearts. Feeding on garbage is a personal choice, and we always look like what we ingest.

In University, we labelled those who begrudged folks their good fortune as *bad belly people*. In my medical school class, really envious and bitter people were deemed to have *peritonitis* which is practically the worse belly ache you could get. This type of painful rotting of the insides makes you scream for the surgeon, undertaker, and local vicar all at once. Every gut has the potential to rupture and release those bad bacteria onto the intestines and its covering peritoneum.

There have been people who went to bed and got woken up by peritonitis in the middle of the night — the enemy within! The mind is like the gut. It must sieve through what looks like good information to extract the good and kick out the junk.

We must take the good with the bad. Food is essential, but it must be digested. The gut is a battlefield where food stays on one side and the digestive enzymes on the other. They fight it out, and the food usually gets it in the neck. All its defences get broken down, and it is stripped away for *parts* which represent the spoils of war. The defeated food army gets flushed down the drain and completely forgotten.

Sometimes, the food sides with allies like Salmonella and win some strategic battles but these are only transient victories. The *house* always wins.

Life is one big fight. The higher occupants of the food chain conquer the minnows and turn them into intestinal residents where every single good thing is sucked out of them to the benefit of their conquerors. The chicken might have had some job satisfaction when laying its egg, but the breakfast table beckons.

Life is not an easy battle. We must manage the war

zones within and stop focussing on external threats all the time. The battles within are constant and needful. Our lives make progress only when we realise we are filled to the eye balls with intestinal residents that must pay rent until they can no longer do so. Then we evict them speedily, making room for the next tenants.

In Summary

There is a constant battle on the inside

If things go wrong on the inside it may be lethal

You must have something to work with: steady input

We take in toxicities without knowing

The quality of our inputs determines our future growth and development

The resident enemies are greater that the external threats; hence friends are close and enemies much closer.

FASTING

THE MOSLEM SEES IT COMING FOR MILES AND plans accordingly. Though some Christian denominations have days of fasting in their calendar, that does not stop impromptu periods of fasting to be declared. Some exclaim, "Jesus!" when the pastor announces that he was *arrested* by the spirit in the dead of the night and commanded to declare a three day fast for the country. Not all members exclaiming "Jesus!" do it in reverence. Some are borderline blasphemous angry folk with visions of that fresh Banga soup that had being earmarked for molestation all week long, aided and abetted by usi (starch) and garri.

These impromptu periods of fasting are always with *immediate effect*. And those are the Sundays that the greedy relative arrives in town unannounced *for his meeting on Monday* On returning home, the kitchen becomes alive with the sounds of food preparation, frying, sizzling, chopping of fish on the chopping board, the blender and soon, there is a request for money to buy Malt for your in-law who cannot drink water like everybody else. A request for money is a polite way to tell you to get into your car and present yourself at Shoprite.

On returning, the Arsenal game is about to kick off (fasting football is not an option). It is pure torture watching matches with *visitors from another church* who are not fasting and who demand nutritional entertainment. The coffee table is decorated with the treble — popcorn, chin chin, and groundnuts. Chin chin is a pacifier for wrong referee decisions. Groundnut is good when bemoaning a wrongly-placed pass while popcorn is the perfect accompaniment to a goal celebration and can double up as a consolation for a disallowed goal or missed chance by the strikers. Nothing is worse than arguing about a disallowed goal in your own living room with a visitor who talks with popcorn in his mouth while you feast on oxygen in the air and swallow spit.

Fasting is important. It is a period when the stomach gets nothing and the spirit excels. This is a time of meditation, contemplation, and prayers with little distraction. The sugar levels do not spike during the fasting period as the body works on energy saved in the past — a bit like going on a long distant flight with a full tank of aviation fuel. Hospitality can be a problem as well as feeding the kids. Absence makes the heart fonder, but the absence of Naija food makes the Naija stomach psychotic. The sense of smell heightens to sniffer dogs level, and Agege bread and akara being eaten miles away can be perceived with ease. Naija food smells a hundred times better than it tastes, and it is a battle not to succumb to the temptation to call off the fast till the next day.

Walking past bread causes auditory hallucinations. "Squeeze me, grab me," the loaves say. The sense of hearing gets selective. Passing lorries and overhead planes are not heard, but the hissing sound of a cold bottled drink being opened across the street is loud, and it startles. The unfortunate poor living in crowded *face-me-face-up* compounds endure the sights and sounds of the neighbours' soups and have to resist the urge to grab the biscuits out of the mouths of the young children in the compound.

Half time and the pounded yam is brought in. Ameidi and Usi follow. The relative says, "Come and join me" and is met with a stern look.

"Oh! I forgot you are fasting. Pray well for us o!"

If I slap person dem go say I wicked. You no think say I know say my wife dey kitchen? If I needed food in my house, I wouldn't go through you.

Human bodies are like modern cars; the hybrid ones that work on fossil fuels and electricity. Two sources of energy to fire the engine. Apart from glucose which fuels the body's functioning, there is fat stored in reserve for when the glucose supplies start to thin out. Once fasting starts, the glucose is soon used up and fat is broken down for energy and the waste product, ketones, gets flushed out of the system via the exhaust pipes. The swap from glucose to fat metabolism sometimes drives one to distraction. Just like *Nepa* striking at 2 a.m., and some poor fellow has to leave the comfort of the bed to go into the rain and switch on the electric generator, all switches of energy supply are never easy. But once the teething problems are overcome, fasting becomes bearable.

The difference between fasting and starvation is initially psychological. In the first few hours, the stomach is just empty, but the one fasting knows he has a full fridge while the starving don't have the idea of where the next meal will come from. The worry and frustration take up all the scarce resources available to the starving, and they lose weight at alarming speeds. Self-inflicted suffering is always easier to manage than an imposed caloric energy intake restriction. A consecrated time of turning one's back on the pleasures of food as part of a spiritual exercise is helped by the supporting belief that profit will come. Hunger, famine or starvation imposed on a person due to bad harvest, war or a draught is psychologically registered as suffering, leading to death and having no benefits whatsoever.

Unfortunately, about one billion people on the planet are seriously hungry with nothing to show in the fridge.

FOOD TOURISM

One day, monkey go market but e no go come back is a well-known Nigerian adage. That the proverbial monkey thought that all the admirers at the City Mall really had its best interest at heart beggars belief. With each shopping trip, the monkey grew more confident and less inclined to attend its ears to the voices of caution and reason. It soon found out that the destiny of the proud was a one-way trip to the land of despair. It ended in ogbono soup surrounded by crustaceans in death. The retail tourist became a victim of food tourists on the prowl.

There are many journeys like going to war that may turn out to be one-way trips. Risky trips fraught with dangers. You either return a hero to be feted by the community or in a body bag inducing grief in the family. Na so monkey rest in pieces.

Food and consumers of food are in constant motion. That is because the yams that can uproot themselves, peel their skin, and dive into hot water without assistance have not been invented. People need to move if they are hungry and don't want to starve.

Some people travel far to eat distant dishes. Foods are also transported to distant lands to tickle the home sick palate. Everyone wants to make it back home ultimately. That is the hope of the gastronomic tourist. They leave a full fridge behind and travel for new dining experiences, but the plan is to return. People tend to return home, but food never comes back, and if it does, it returns with a foreign accent. Like the cocoa that returns as chocolate that is now too posh to grace the tables of the poor farmers that saw it through infancy to adulthood.

Nigerian people will always deny that they think of the food they will eat at arrival as they pack their suitcases and reach for the passport and airline ticket, but the Naija Food Philosopher reads minds. People lick their lips as they board planes to the motherland. Not in anticipation of the *fish or chicken* offered in tiny packages on the planes. No. Hunger on arrival means appetite on arrival. At the final destination which is the family homestead, before the gates are opened (always a problem finding the right padlock key in the darkness), the aroma from the kitchen drifts out in freedom to say, "Welcome, sir. We dey wait you." The mosquitoes also say hello, but they are waved away with disdain. Missing home is really all a cover up for missing food. I have seen flights into Nigeria from the UK and flights out of Nigeria back to base. The seat belts always need to be adjusted when flying out of Nigeria *as the belle don increase.*

Food is beautiful and should be eaten without guilt or apologies. Food is not a tablet to be taken at the exact time and at the same dose daily. Food is a cultural experience best imbibed surrounded by people who know the culture (wey sabi). A plate of food is always sweeter when everyone in a twenty five mile radius will rush at the plate if you decide not to eat anymore. It's that trophy wife syndrome!

Don't you wish your fufu was fine like mine. Don't ya!

People travel with their food choices in this global village we live in. That means they would set up restaurants anywhere they stop travelling and build a home. That means the guys with a wandering palate do not need to fly to a foreign land to eat something foreign. What is an exotic country if not the food and music? These can be created in a restaurant saving money and the plane ticket costs. The taste and texture of the food in a place accounts for a majority of the nostalgic memories there are. Chinese, Indian, Italian, and African restaurants exist in all the big cities on the planet. The gastronomic tourist goes on the prowl with the cuisine being the compass that informs the choice of destination. There is no compass like a delightful plate of food.

Despite the huge number of international journeys embarked upon stemming from gut feelings, the local and regional tourists far outweigh the passport-carrying tourists.

All invitations to dinner are usually accepted based on culinary expectations. Once bitten, twice shy after all. Why honour an invitation for one hour and eat N8K worth of hospitality only to develop an alimentary malady necessitating a five-day hospital admission and a handsome bill of N400K? Before dressing up and turning up as a guest, one must be sure that the hostess knows the difference between raw and well-cooked chicken. The chef must have also taken out time to know the finer distinguishing points between Atlantic sea water and pepper soup.

It would be improper to mention names, but there are people who would invite me out to dinner and make me turn up like a universal recipient with a Kilimanjaro appetite, while some other invites would tempt me to exhibit a lying spirit — on call that day (I cannot come and keee myself because of politeness).

Everybody does it. The food is what comes to mind

when contemplating any outing. Some arm themselves with a full stomach as insurance is better than complaints. Too little salt is ok, but who can stand drinking Dead Sea juice as a starter or incinerated dodo branded as Chargrilled plantain.

Up till now, I have presumed the tourist is a normal physiological human being. The type with an average height, weight, and appetite. There are the ones who indulge in local tourism in restaurants where they pay their fee or in homes they have been invited to. There is, however, a special breed of visitors who like James Bond, 007 do not wait for a visa or invite to turn up. These secret agents who believe they have been licenced to eat and drink you dry by the powers that be just turn up and look you in the eyes daring you not to offer them *something*. These ones have the stomachs of vultures and the temerity of oxen that grew up with goats. Tell them that you think your stew has gone off, and they will tell you to bring the pot. They will devour the whole lot oblivious to the incredulous looks being bestowed on them. These are the ones for which you get in your car for an enforced holiday if they tell you they are in your area (sometimes they are packed outside and have seen your car already). The vulture is nature's ultimate food tourist. It hasn't the hustle to fight or kill, so it just waits for free food, and beggars have no choice. Rotten flesh? Well, food na food.

The food espionage guys are dining table surfers. When you run out of salt, they reach into their pocket and bring out their supply. Their gluttony is part vice and part talent — skill and greed in harmony.

NAIJA FOOD PHILOSOPHER

THE THING THAT HAS BEEN IS WHAT WILL BE again. The blue plastic bowl was bought to make eba. Each night, the garri was poured into the boiling water in the blue plastic bowl and stirred with a wooden spatula. Then there was too much garri in the hot water to permit an easy stirring, so the hard task of mixing the eba begins. Soon, the eba is ready and put in a plate. It has been true down the ages: hot water and garri makes eba.

In the spirit of procrastination, the dirty bowl is filled with water rather than washing it. This is to soak and soften the garri and make washing easier. The bowl is washed the next day only to start the cycle again. Mouths to feed never cease, and food preparation goes on and on. You see it from the beginning of the raining season to the dry season. It features from the festive naming ceremonies, to the weddings and then the funerals. The wonderful soups from the east and the glorious soups from the west all assemble on tables. There are so many scenarios, but the garri keeps on being both constant and relevant.

The fool eats garri, and the wise eats the same. It serves the Oba's Palace and is the star staple in the labourers' camp. Plates may vary in style and quality, but eba remains eba just as air remains air in every nostril on earth.

Garri does not come easy under the sun. A handful of hot eba in hand is worth twenty in the fancy restaurant in the sluggard's mind. Cassava is planted in toil and harvested in the heat of the day. Out of it comes the garri after much labour, yet the wicked people desire to pour sand in the garri of the righteous. So what is the use of gathering mountains of garri in sacks? You eat and eat and die. Then your mourners arrive with appetites. They sing dirges till they are too weak to sing and have to be revived by garri while the star of the show lies in a wooden box watching people he hates eat all his garri. He feels like standing up and walking over to spit in their soups, but he too ate the garri of the other deceased people who went before him.

There is nothing new under the sun; we take turns. I eat your obito garri, and your children later eat mine. Brief illness finally catches up with everybody. It is a vanity to work so hard for garri, but work we must.

So arise and hustle for your hunger will come, and they are not sharing free garri anywhere.

What a *vexation of spirit!*

I hated all my labour in which I have toiled under the sun, seeing that I must leave this garri *to the man who will succeed me. Who knows if he would be wise or a fool?*

There are times to listen to the Rolex and at other times one must smell what the Timex is cooking in the chronometer. All creatures, great and small, under the heavens must discern what season they have woken up into. There is a time to soak garri with G units and there is a time to eat garri *dry* with the garri laying on its back and thinking of Nigeria while sugar gets sprinkled all over it. There is a time to have the ice blocks laidback and garri gets sprinkled all over it, and there is a time to be conservative and prove the theorem true that water and garri make eba. There is a time for ogbono to engage the garri and there is a time for owo soup. There is a day for white garri and soon, the day for yellow garri arrives. There is a day to hide the eba and swallow spit till that visitor goes, and there is a time to share one's food with the brethren. There is a time when the mouth will not open to admit garri, despite the garri passing JAMB, and there is a time to open the mouth wide. Only a fool attempts to drink garri daily, and if he has no friends to dissuade him, kwashiorkor would be his best friend.

It is vanity for the bread winner to lose his appetite, and the hired chef takes the *chop remain* home and enjoys a joyous feast with his family. It is madness to be in an expensive bed with insomnia having refused to eat garri which was passed to the family dog who ate so well it is sound asleep. Many on silk sheets surrounded by air-conditioners but with no inner peace-conditioners toss and turn as they wrestle anorexia and insomnia while the fridge is over flowing with food. Not everyone eating their garri is laughing. Some turn their garri around in the okra soup wishing they had different company. That is vanity. Loneliness is evil. Steaming eba eaten without soup is like living a life without companions. Eba needs to be dipped in something dissimilar. Eba cannot excel dipped in eba, no matter the quality of the garri.

The heart must be with the garri. Don't swallow you eba wishing for jollof in your heart lest the eba chokes you. Eba in hand is worth a million fantasies in Banana Island. Hold the one wey reach your hand and enjoy am like the last meal you go chop for this life. The garri enters the hot water naked, but dem wrap am plastic put for plate. Oga, naked the eba, baptise am for owo soup come swallow am. Naked through the gut until it sees light at the end of a stinking tunnel and falls out naked. Everybody is like garri—come in naked, wear cloth small, then go back naked. Between coming and going is the life; let us pray that as we make our eba, so shall we enjoy it. If you make am anyhow, you go chop am anyhow.

There is no tomorrow coming when one would retire and enjoy eba. Enjoy the one in front of you today for who knows tomorrow. In the days of youth, when the teeth are not bought and the taste buds not retired, that is when to chop up and live up. When the sugar level is low and the blood pressure is lower. Everybody will die, whether they eat one hand of eba or four. Whether they don't like cassava or shun those with big cassava, everyone is going. So relish your food in the morning, and at lunch, have a celebratory feast. There is no need to worry about tomorrow when your Egusi is in position like a penalty kick you must take.

If a man will live many days, let him know that tears will be shed on many. In between the sad days, mould that eba well, dunk it in a soup and open wide with joy. It is the Lord's doing, and it is marvellous to our taste buds.

Food is Ready

Come in quick. Food is ready
Rest, drink. I see your hard life
written on your brow. Come in,
sit. There is so much to say.

You brought your paintings home
but had no father to admire
You have fought alone. Like an orphan.
The battle's over. Eat what you desire

Come home. Let the healing begin
Come in from the cold. The insecurities.
Listen. First there is love, sweet love.
No more loneliness. No disharmony.

You threw away your crayons and your heart
There is a stone where the heart should be
You felt a heart of stone will not be broken
You are right. But the stone cannot love.

Come in, a change of heart awaits
You did not feel good enough. Beautiful enough
That low self-esteem is all gone
Come in and taste the love

LOST WITHOUT TRACE

A WORKMAN IS ONLY AS GOOD AS THE TOOLS he has to work with. I must have been about six or seven when my father decided his children needed cutlery sets with their initials engraved on them. This was both a gift and a trap for you dare not turn up at the dinner table without your personalised tools. Alas, with time, the utensils disappeared, and it would have been totally impossible for anyone to suggest a place that Sherlock Holmes could start the investigations for their recovery even if he was brought back from his fictional resting place. That same Bermuda Triangle that roamed across Nigeria while on holiday making monthly menstrual periods disappear thereby causing a population explosion in its wake also had designs on our dinner table utensils.

Like a dark cloud that hung over the nation, this triangle took life and properties with ease. Fela sang about the unknown soldier, police, and civilian which all added up to an unknown government. I suspect it was this Bermuda triangle that is wreaking havoc. In boarding school in Kaduna, I had a junior student who brought my cutlery set to the dining hall and gave them to me. He came after eating to collect the set for washing (a form one boy sent to school for academic development). Why I couldn't just carry my own shining silver service by myself I would never know.

One day, I found him bewildered. He looked after six seniors and had gotten all their utensils mixed up. He had lost mine and was holding the last set which was meant for him. He cried to the teacher when I took his to eat with. I got a warning and lost my utensils. That triangle of evil had struck again.

Unfortunately for me, I have been unable to lose that cloud that steals cutlery in every house I have ever lived in. You buy a shining selection of plates which may be anything from 32 to 40 pieces, and slowly but surely the population dwindles till you are left with just one bowl. You suspect that those who live with you are selling choice plates on eBay, but you just cannot prove it.

The cutlery set is sweetest to use on the first day. Absolutely new and shining, you see your reflection on the concave spoon before diving into the hot stew. Like after the honeymoon period, it is downhill from then on. The teaspoons always go first. From six to one and then suddenly you notice two teaspoons that were not even in the original set. Perhaps there might be a sort of redistribution process by the Bermuda triangle evil spirits.

Next, the spoons start to go down in number. Those with children blame them. I once had to open a video recorder that stopped working only to find a spoon, knife, and fork. Very young children love to throw things in the bin. After the yoghurt is gone, sending them to "throw it away" could lead to both the empty plastic container and the spoon going into the bin. One of my kids once loved throwing utensils and plantain out of the first floor kitchen window. This landed in a garden I didn't have access to. We found out by chance when we caught the perpetrator in the act.

Family members who eat in their rooms sometimes would prefer either forks or spoons. The type of person who takes food to the bedroom usually would not take a full complement of cutlery on a tray to the room and then return promptly to wash the dishes as soon as the meal is finished. Rather, the plate might be held in transit for one to two days and finally returned to the kitchen with the spoon left somewhere under the bed as a holiday home for fungi and bacteria. In the end, you can be left with six knives and nothing else. To avoid this from happening, a new cutlery set is bought. When that happens, the family rushes to the new shining utensils ignoring the old and the Bermuda triangle strikes. With time, the population of the old and new utensils are the same.

It is inevitable that things will get lost in Nigeria and in Nigerian homes. That is probably why salaries should be paid monthly. There is always need to stock up on food and cutlery. The breakdown of home appliances sometimes reunites you with teaspoons long forgotten. The electrician comes in and pulls out the fridge and there are spoons everywhere. Moving house is the ultimate revelation of lost things. There are always cutlery and coins to be picked up when the cupboards get moved.

Unfortunately, some people are just thieves. They visit you for the night and steal cutlery. We once had a relative stay with us for a few months and the night before his departure, my mum went through his bags without a warrant. That bag packed in so much Bermuda triangle capabilities it could have housed the snake that swallowed the N36 million naira. There was nothing he had not stolen. From cutleries to family photographs he was not even in. Perfumes, bars of soap, and various trivial that showed he had been save-stealing for up to a month prior to his departure date. He deserved an Oscar for actually stealing the envelope with his name written on it that contained the money which was his farewell gift. He must have hoped that my dad would have searched in vain for the envelope and then given him the money out of his wallet.

So long as there is that sweet aroma of food there would be cutlery waiting for skilful hands to work that magic of eating for sustenance and enjoyment. There has to be a better way for one cannot condemn the next generation to this losing culture of today. This year alone, apart from losses Nigeria has endured in the brain drain department, there has been football match losses, national revenue disappearances, and even more monthly menstrual periods vanishing thus consigning us to that position of the most populated place in Africa.

The only way forward is to embrace technology — cutlery with computer chips so that they can be tracked electronically. That way, when food is ready and there are only knives around, the smart phone can locate where the Bermuda Triangle spirits have hidden the rest of the cutlery.

THE GREATEST PLATE OF MY LIFE

IT IS ROUND AND WEIGHTY. YOU PLACE IT IN front of you. You take a deep breath. Step back a bit, and then you move forward with that look of determination in the eyes. That is how a penalty kick is taken. And that is how history is made. The same applies to food. There are some epic meals that have been set before me that cannot be forgotten, and this is my trip down memory lane, recounting the greatest plates of my life.

You know what a great plate is. The ones that make you glad to be at the table even before you taste the food. You are inspired to float in a sea of gratitude for the meal that has been placed before you. Quite unlike those other plates that can be best described as a trial of your faith. You know the ones. Naija people would pray lengthy prayers imploring God to kill any bacteria on the plate and detoxify any poisons contained therein (both physical and spiritual) when the food does not look particularly well-endowed with attractiveness.

Nay! Today we talk only about the sweet memories of when the tongue tasted morsels of heaven on earth.

Talking about the tongue, one must give it accolades. That is the only place where one can taste food (although greedy people seem to taste food with their hearts, eyes, and noses). The sole provider of the pleasures derived from food is the tongue. It is also one of the few organs of pleasure that serves humans into old age. Eyes may need glasses and the ears may need hearing aids, but the Naija tongue just keeps on licking that ogbono forever. Well, after fifty years of age, the taste buds start to become less effective but like we say in my village, when the multi-millionaire loses twenty percent of his income, he is still very rich.

Two thirds of the tongue has those tantalising sensations transported to the brain via the facial nerve and the back third goes via the glossopharyngeal nerve. A bit like one man having calls coming through both his Glo and his MTN phones. The messages from the tongue all end up in the gustatory area of the brain and if the stimulation is intense enough, the memory is filed away permanently.

I think my earliest great plate was one of those

breakfast bonanzas at Falolu Road. My dad has been to Leventis and returned with cartons of food.

Fried sausages, eggs, bacon, bread, and strawberry jam filled the table as did the Kellogg's cornflakes and milk. We ate to bursting point and then ate some more. There were many breakfast tables like this, but I recall one particular occasion when the planets were all in alignment, and the food tasted divine. One swallowed with a sense of history, almost as if one was representing the country in the swallowing Olympics. It must have been in 1972, when most days were summer days. The sizzling sausages sent a delicious aroma all over the house and even went through the windows to pepper the neighbours. My young body began to act like a cat fish that had the capacity to taste the food all over my skin. Not sure I have eaten any breakfast like that ever since. Over the years I have had my first meals of the day on boats, planes, trains, and even while out, running (about 17, 000 breakfast meals), but nothing compares to that Falolu extravaganza.

The sweets soon came daily. Tom-tom and goody-goody echoed in my pockets but no satisfaction. That was until I was invited to a particular four to six. Those were the evening birthday parties where one donned the Sunday best for a weekday party. I remember vividly wearing my flared trousers and brand new shoes and taking my seat on that collapsible wooden chair everyone in Surulere seemed to hire for parties. My food came on a paper plate, and it was jollof rice, moin-moin, cubes of hard dodo, and stewed beef. I looked down and kept on eating without a care in the world. That discovery of the pure white flesh of a boiled egg in my moin-moin was a delightful encounter. The beef was both chewy and tasty, but I had a full set of teeth back then in 1974 and so could chew myself into a labyrinth of happiness and subsequently chew my way back out. Those were the days when a piece of meat that felt too big for its boots was converted into chewing gum (via persistent mastication) and swallowed two hours later.

My first buka experience was with a neighbour's driver. He had dropped the kids at school and was giving me a lift to my bus stop, but we got side-tracked by hunger. It was somewhere in Yaba close to Herbert Macaulay Way. The place was full of men who had left home too early to eat. The menu was set. Steaming rice, boiled blacked-eye beans, and dodo that was fried incompletely. The stew and meat could raise the dead in the local Atan Cemetery if the wind took the aroma that far. I always had breakfast before leaving home and my dad was particularly against "eating outside", so this buka trip was a crime which added to the excitement. Naturally, the stew differed from what you got at home. Generally speaking, Naija women hardly changed how they make their food, so you get accustomed to home food. A Naija friend once said he could identify his wife's soup out of an identity parade of ten dishes. In addition, he could tell her state of mind at the time of cooking!

When you are used to the same soup every night, that vagabond tongue rejoices at the novelty of new sensations.

It was almost a matter of time before the inevitable happened. In 1977 on a Sunday morning, there was the Ukodo to remember. It was a family meal just before we left for church. Hot and straight to the point. Yams, dry fish, pepper soup with that unsung hero, bright red palm oil. It was a meal fit for a king. I had eaten many Ukodo meals before and many afterwards, but this one marked my brain with indelible digital ink.

But here is a thought. What if my greatest plate is yet to come? What if it is more important to do all I can to make my daily bread my best meal ever? Isn't the greatest plate the next one you are alive to sit in front of and eat?

PLATE ENVY

THE LOVE FOR ANOTHER MAN'S FOOD IS A special kind of greed. You see it in parties when people are in queues, and the lady holding the spoon smiles affectionately at a guy holding a plate and then piles a lot of Jollof rice on his plate while maintaining her smile. The smile evaporates when the next "unknown" guy holds out his plate. She plays golf with the surface grains of rice in a back and forth motion, then turns pit digger thrusting the spoon deep into the rice holding the hungry man's heart in her spoon. She then shakes the spoon and converts the mountain to a plain and puts the tiny portion on the plate. The man asks for more, and she gives him *that look* then dives into the rice while maintaining her eye contact with him. With that glance, only Nigerian men understand.

You no get wife for house wey go cook for you? Her eyes say. She gives the second spoon and looks at the next man indicating time is up. This is when the poor guy looks at his plate and looks at the plate of the man going in front of him, and the envious feelings well up.

It is the same in the bukas where the definition of *one spoon of rice* is interpreted by the hands of the one who holds the spoon. This subjective weighing of food is not fair and some guys, the fine boys, the big boys and the charismatic boys might as well say, *na dem dey rush us,* for they get back-to-back lion shares of all food items.

In Nigerian weddings, everyone looks at the plate of his neighbours as he or she walks back to their seat. This breeds envy that gets compounded when the souvenir lady walks around with that who-know-man App in her eyes and serves the gift items according to Aso Ebi status or according to how much she likes your face. Human beings don't like the fact that some people seem to get more than others in all aspects of life.

One guy, a few years ago, visited his brother's house at meal time (what a coincidence) and naturally was invited for lunch. He was later to lament that *our wife* gave her mother who was also visiting at the time four large pieces of meat, and he was given two pieces of meat with some miserable four shrimps that looked like they had been deported from Europe (not imported o). He actually was counting pieces of meat on someone else's plate. His conclusion was that "this wife dey chop all my brother money." I felt like giving him that look: *You no get wife for house wey go cook for you*? But I was young and feared for my life. A man over forty that is involved in a meat census on someone else's plate in someone else's house is capable of murder.

It is a fact of life that some people will be getting bigger and better than others. While it is understandable that a man who lives in an airless oven might notice the difference when he visits the air conditioned residence of his fellow man, it is reasonable to expect that he should be happy that only one of them has to live in an oven. And when that same man walks past the family dog and sees a fat piece of chicken that he would rather have, it is not the dog's fault. Plates of food look good on Instagram, but that does not mean it tastes better than what anyone has in their homes. True, the salad is always greener on social media and there is an allure for the plate that is beyond reach. However, it might be full of salt or cold and badly prepared.

Those in films seem to eat and tell the best jokes and look happier than what pertains at real life dinner tables. Well, the jokes are scripted, and these are actors pretending to love each other. The ice cubes in the drinks are plastic cubes that wouldn't melt under the hot lights as the director commands them to repeat the scene on end. All that dining room beauty is just Hollywood make-believe.

Nothing is sweeter than the food you did not cook. You just turn up, take a seat with the speed of a horse, smell that wonderful aroma and salivate like a pig and then start eating like a horse. At the end, you leave without clearing the table or washing the dishes. I guess that is why restaurants were invented. The problem is when someone else's personal home is treated like a restaurant, especially when they are great cooks.

Some visitors time their visits to perfection, causing the sages of old to invent that greeting that is usually accompanied with a hypocritical smile: "You meet me well my brother, wash hand." It is only well for the visitor because the plate owner had planned to eat in peace, listening to Celestine Ukwu and reserving that roast fish for the end of the meal. Now the fish has to be offered up as sacrifice on the altar of hospitality. He prays a bone chokes the visitor as he smiles and passes sixty percent of his fish to him.

When thou sittest to eat with a ruler, consider diligently what is before thee:

And put a knife to thy throat, if thou be a man given to appetite.
Be not desirous of his dainties: for they are deceitful meat.

There is no better plate than the one in front of man. That is the meal to be grateful for. Imagine those who were envious of the affluent families living large in Manhattan in 1903. These rich folk had a cook called Mary Mallon otherwise known as Typhoid Mary. She cooked well but added typhoid-causing germs to each plate for she carried the germs in her body. Many took ill and three died during the course of her career.

Awoof dey run purge (other people's delicacies are liable to provoke gastrointestinal maladies). When it came to big hype about food, none could rival the Titanic. Those with great talents in lusting for food they could never afford had in the description of the Titanic's culinary arrangements a real life fantasy. First class passengers were practically in heaven, and they had the best utensils and wines. Over thirty chefs worked hard to produce the best food on a floating vessel since Noah fed his animals in the Ark.

This floating wonder left Southampton on the tenth of April 1912 amidst fanfare but in the end, all the plate envy turned out to be a vanity. Luther Vandross put it so well when he sang about love, and it works well with food: *If you can't be with the one you love, love the one you are with.*

MUSICAL PLATES

NIGERIAN JOLLOF WAS MADE FOR MUSIC AS was all the other Naija foods. Pepper soup in a steamy bowl congested with assorted floating and submerged edibles is best swallowed with Peacocks International Guitar band, playing the guitar that makes one forget the problems of life and slurp away happily. The Eddie Quansah song drowns out the noisy eating habits of your neighbour and prevents the panic when pepper goes the wrong way and someone starts choking. "Bros, drink water," someone says, passes a glass, and pats him on the back. Once the danger has passed, someone else teases, "Your village people don start again o."

There are some Nigerian foods that would refuse to go down the gullet without music, especially if more than twenty people are present. I recall eating at a party when the music stopped, and all we had was the clinking of cutlery, chewing noises, coughing, and noisy conversation enveloping us with an unpleasant sound cloud and sonic drizzle. The silence was unbearable, and many stopped eating.

Love, music, and food all get along fine in the Naija ecosystem. The musicians are not oblivious to this fact, and the food references abound in the Naija music that we all love.

Oni dodo oni moin-moin is a Yoruba folk song that has been covered both by Fela Kuti and Sam Apkabot at different times. That song floods my mind with visions of hot rice, slices of dodo, and moin-moin all baptised with the sprinkling upon of hot bright red tomato stew. Dodo is one of my favourite foods, and the way the song emphasises the sound *dodo* makes the Naija mouth water. Fresh Dodo can never keep a secret of its presence. It could be fried at the east end of the street, and the smell travels through the air, tormenting each house until it gets to the other end of the street and dances back.

Moin-moin is made from ground beans, and beans features in another Yoruba folk song that went thus:

There is oil, there is beans
I am not afraid to have twins
Because there is oil, there is beans

Now what is better than a rice and beans orchestra? The thoughts that these song evoke produce dancing vibrations in the soul. Bunny Mack was from Sierra

Leone, but his monster hit, *Let me love you* was loved and adopted by Nigerians.

> *You are my sweetie my sugar*
> *My baby My lover*

In my youth, when I saw nothing wrong in chewing on a cube of St Louis or Tate sugar, this song struck a chord. Gone are those days of blissful ignorance when I had no diabetic patients or education. In recent times, my ability to cope with spices has waned, and I avoid Shito at all costs. Just looking at it in a jar takes my gastric pH southwards, but I love the wonderful personal irony when I get all emotional on hearing Runtown's *Mad over you:*

> *Ghana girl, say she wan marry me o*
> *I hope say she sabi cook waakye*
> *Hope your love go sweet pass shito*

Hmmm, sounds like pure reflux oesophagitis love to me. Another ironic twist is from none other than the Kokomaster himself who equated his *hotness to hot amala to ji na gaan gaan* in the song *Gbono Feli Feli.* Now, I am not an amala eater, but I feel good about the song to date. And sometimes, when I am really feeling myself, I think, *Hmmmm! African Michael Jackson!* Na dem dey rush us!

Nothing is as attractive as hot food. After all, the

salesmen tell us that good merchandise sells like hot cake. Newer sounds like Solid star and Tiwa Star sing about *Baby Jollof my love, you too sweet like jollof.* These singers make me wonder if a girl can be *sweet* like Nigerian jollof. Hmmm, expectations should be kept attainable, please.

When Duncan Mighty sang in the studio with Tiwa Savage in the song *Lova Lova,* I wonder if it was real love or hunger:

> *This your love sweet, Ofada Rice*
> *Nne you too Sweet like a Yam Porridge.*

Indomie's ubiquitous nature is referenced in Burna Boy's Killin Dem featuring Zlatan:

> *Wo ni elo ni*
> *Making money rush rush like Indomie*

And not to be out done, Teni professed undying love by promising to endure poverty just to be with the one she loves in the song case. After establishing that her lineage does not include Dangote or Adeleke families, she suggests a potential weekly menu:

> *So tell me, what the hell are you waiting for?*
>
> *If na to chop Indomie, we go chop*
> *If na to soak e Garri, we go soak*
> *What the hell are you waiting for*
> *If na to fry Akara we go fry*

If na to soak Akamu we go soak

Now to the elephant in the room. You cannot go four songs on any Naija play list without thinking all music recording studios in Nigeria are located on a plantation or on Banana Island. There is an epidemic of banana references which risks flooding the ears with potassium. This phase will pass hopefully, and I am not a big fan of banana music. Well, I used to be when Dan-I recorded *Monkey Chop*. It was a big hit in the seventies, and the chorus was everywhere: *Monkey, come chop banana.*

I still don't understand the song till now. *But* when it comes to love songs and food, the best example is down to the Kokomaster, Dbanj:

When the Kokomaster fall in love
You know say water don pass Garri
My sweet Potato
I wanna tell you my mind
My Sugar banana
As I don get you if I say make I hammer

I am not quite sure what the recipe for sugar banana is, but I guess the Kokomaster has some form of Gastronomic Immunity and artistic licence in that kitchen of his.

There is no doubt that music can affect our emotional states and modify our food-seeking behaviour, especially in groups. In parties with very good DJs, people dance for hours, and the drinks and food always run out. Fast-paced music *gingers* people, and they, in turn, expend more energy. They sweat more and drink more. Even when eating alone, I tend to play some music. Listening to the humming of the fridge or electric generator and air conditioners (depending on which country I am in) is bad for eating. On flights, the depressing white noise that aircraft engines give off is replaced with the in-flight entertainment. The meals are usually nothing to fly home about, but I guess that is why everyone is given headphones at the beginning of the flight.

In all matters of the stomach, just as it is with love, ambience is paramount. And the quickest way to set the mood is via music.

> *If music be the food of love, play on;*
> *Give me excess of it, that, surfeiting,*
> *The appetite may sicken, and so die.*

GELATO

THE ICONIC FOODS TRENDING IN THE MINDS and social media platforms of Nigerians are what we all expect: kola nuts, wedding cakes, jollof rice, birthday cakes, garri, and a totally new comer — gelato ice cream.

Nigeria is a hot country, and ice lollies after school was how I grew up. There were cyclists carrying ice boxes in front of their bicycles at our primary school gate, sweating in the midday heat and looking like they needed their merchandise more than us. Fan Ice cream was the popular brand, and its unmistakable logo was painted on the bicycle. There was an aperture at the top of their ice boxes which they opened to take out ice cream, and we all looked in to see the ice and feel the cold mist rise up. It was like peeping into heaven through a window in hell. The ice cream cyclist came armed with a sharp razor blade in case two pupils needed to buy one vanilla ice cream and have it split in to two. Samco was another brand that made cartooned milk, yoghurt, and chocolate drinks. Popsicle sticks ice-cream, some being *double-barrelled, lending* itself to sharing. The ice cream sticks were collected and used to make boomerangs that never could fly back once despatched.

Ice lollies were also popular, but the daddy of them all was the big dip — an ice cream on a wooden stick plated in 24 carat chocolate. It seemed to make one taller after eating one under the mischievous tropical sun that attempted to cook us every afternoon with little success. This was in the 70s. Pupils had disposable income, and we ate and licked away on our iced delicacies-loving life in the country we were taught to believe was the Giant of Africa.

We were giants in licking ice cream. Even after school, the cyclists came to our neighbourhoods, ringing their bells and screaming, "Walls ice cream! Chocolate! Banana! Ice creammm!" We rushed downstairs to stop them. Around 1974, one of the ice cream cyclists felt bicycles were below our station, and he imported a brand new ice cream van complete with the loudest ding dong sounding music that drew out the kids like the Pied Piper of Hamelin. Parents expanded with pride as their kids *chopped and licked their* proverbial money. Vanilla on a cone or chocolate in a cone.

Life was good. Memories of shared moments, eating with parents never leave the mind. The standard meals of breakfast, lunch, and supper have a certain routine that makes the meals easy to forget. It is, after all, the child's right to be fed, and daddy's job was essentially to put bread on the table or perhaps bring home the bacon. When the bread and bacon comes, it is soon forgotten but not so with ice cream. Snacks were not in the contract and any sweet-tasting edible beauties eaten came as a privilege, not a right. Fathers usually don't put ice cream on the proverbial table, so when they do, one remembers. The same also is true for those with fathers who could not buy the ice cream as a result of absence or poverty. The kids grow up never forgetting, and some unfortunately become gluttons trying to claw back all they had missed in childhood at great risks to their health.

It was a shame when successive military regimes converted Naija from the land of milk and honey into a land of ponmo and no-money that devoured its inhabitants. Enter the 80s, and we outgrew ice cream, opting for suya when money was available.

Ice cream never featured in much of Naija music during the ponmo and no-money years. But recently, things have changed. It started with a viral video of a Nigerian businessman and his daughter, DJ Cuppy, licking gelato during an alleged one-hour stopover in Italy. The popularity of the gelato clip culminated in a song being released by DJ Cuppy, featuring Zlatan entitled *Gelato*.

It is a fun novelty song, but that family connection features heavily:

"Who's your daddy?"
"Otedola"

That was so poignant. It took me back to asking for ice cream money at home. The pride a father has when he feeds his own children their favourite snacks. The video is a kaleidoscope of sorts. It just makes you want to have fun, forget calorie counting and gorge on gelato for a day. But my problem has always been overthinking. The Naija Food Philosopher pontificates on fathers who cannot buy bread let alone ice cream in today's world. I read that Nigeria's cattle population is fifteen million. So surely, these cows should be able to produce milk that can be made into affordable gelato for the young kids who have worked hard in school and braved the aggressive sunshine on the way back home (even the ten million children who have never seen the inside of a classroom deserve some gelato).

If Luther Vandross had been born in Surulere, things might have been different with his hit song

Dance with my father. Dance ke?

More like eat with my Father, go and tell him food is ready or hang around in orbit in case he cannot finish the meat. The link between a Naija child and his father is purely via the oesophagus. Then there is the collection of school fees. Or how else would the child be a doctor, lawyer or engineer?

In today's Nigeria, maybe we need more cows. Not conflict cows and herdsmen that lead to the death of citizens but generous cows making Naija the land of milk it was before (last last, we can cope without honey).

Gelato is an Italian word for ice cream. Gelato is different as it contains less air and so is denser than normal ice cream due to the manufacturing process. Although it originates in Italy, it can be made anywhere in the world.

Due to the popularity of the Gelato song by DJ Cuppy, a strange situation has arisen whereby more Nigerians have enjoyed gelato with their ears than those who have enjoyed it with their mouths.

Kola nuts, wedding cakes, jollof rice, birthday cakes, and garri remain the iconic items of foods that people really eat.

NAIJA UNITED FC

YES, THE NAIJA UNITED FOOD CLUB IN WEST africa is more epic than the Kilimanjaro of East Africa. Naija for life: we play to belleful. We die here; no transfer requests and no selling of players. Some might go on loan for a time, two times or three times, but that gastronomic agaracha always wanders home, sniffing that egusi trail.

Nigerians are united in their hunger for the beautiful essentials of life. "Water, food, light and houses" as *the Black President* pronounced. To that, we add air for like water, air no get enemy.

People have voiced their opinions about the magnetic bond that holds Nigeria together; the way unrelated and dissimilar bits of metal are stuck to a giant magnet. What is that tie that binds the Ondo soccer lover to the Kaduna exotic car lover? Some have said it is religion. Even though one hundred percent of Naijaz rush for air, there is no religion with a unanimously high uptake. The Super Eagles, when winning important games, draw people together around their TVs for such is the power of football in sub-Saharan Africa.

Football indeed binds Naija people but even as popular as the *tapping of leather is*, the game is not everybody's cup of tombo. Parables of a people are telling. Naijaz will say, "Man must wack", *meaning* a man must eat and then go hustle to get tomorrow's morsel of food through parted lips.

Food binds us in Nigeria. I think it is high time the horses and eagle on our coat of arms were replaced with yams, cassava, and chicken. Cassava rules in Nigeria. The bigger the cassava the better the garri. Garri cuts across every boundary in Nigeria — real or imagined.

The Naira and its management is a widely-held vocation by the people. We rise, thinking about naira and go to bed, holding it close to our hearts. The loyalty is, however, short-lived in as high as eighty percent of the population, especially the men. A skilful guitarist only needs to sing one stanza of praises, and people will empty their pockets of hard-earned (or hard-stolen) naira, spraying liquidated cash for water no get enemy. A voluptuous human being walks past, and many reach for their cheque books, imploring her to "chop their money." Soon the naira flees, and the big man joins the fast-growing I-used-to-have-money club.

But try testing loyalty with hot beans on soft bread on a cold harmattan morning. Add a bit of native stew (whatever that means) to the summit of beans, and Naijaz will display a one hundred percent loyalty rate. Salivation is usually so much that the beans experiences a bit of white water rafting in the Naija mouth followed by the tunnel vision of the Naija oesophagus. Even though we are ruled by the same President, he has not got the majority in the opinion polls of our hearts the way hot beans does. As for dodo, moin-moin, and jollof rice, these are the perennial three wise men that return again and again, bringing us together on the same hymn sheet party after party. Just say jollof rice, and the whole Naija world smiles with you. In addition to the air we breathe, days of death and birthdays are owned by all Nigerians, even if there are no certificates to prove we were born or had succumbed to a *brief illness.* (Who certificate epp?)

Amala and abula unite the west; starch sticks the Niger-Delta together. Abacha, the salad, is much loved in the east, and tuwo shinkafa is a crowd-favourite up north. Elections may have forty percent registration in geopolitical zones, but these foods score one hundred percent compliance in their corresponding geo-nutritional zones. Afrobeat and Nollywood that battle for Nigerians' ears and eyes cannot battle rice and, most definitely, are no match for suya on a grill on a cool harmattan night. Gulder, star beer, and small stout — another trio of wise bottles make Nigeria have the highest number of alcohol drinkers in Africa. Pot bellies (tortoise under the shirt) confirms Naija's bottle census superiority. Alcohol flows in more veins than plasmodium falciparum or the bad haemorrhagic fever viruses. Naija United Food Club players like to wash things down south just the way the country washes everything via the Niger and Benue rivers into the Niger Delta.

Food is the tie that binds. The popular music is only tolerated because drinks and food are anticipated. Most Naija stars have voices that irritate people with an empty stomach. The truly hungry can cope with gospel music that cultivates hope for the next plate. Wedding receptions are endured for food and drink. Try staging a funeral without food and drink, and you might find yourself alone with the departed. For some countries, their census periods unite the country in a numerical solidarity, but not so in Nigeria where everyone is not counted. The tax man understands this for he knows bottle groundnuts and gala have a higher chance of reaching all the citizens than tax bills.

With an increasing population, some might postulate that sex is the national past time, but that is far from the truth. The man came for the food, and one plate led to another until the belleful people stumbled on the *ozzaaa* room. Drinks, namely star larger, ogogoro, and small stout account for Nigeria's population explosion, not love, lust and other things in-between.

No bi persin wey chop belleful dey indulge in dangerous play?

The various palaces nationwide kid themselves about how popular yearly festivals are to the indigenes, and no cost is spared in staging regattas, durbars, masquerades, native wrestling shows, and maiden dances. The crowd is there for the food. Naija people love that great *point and kill* fantasy — the Argungu Fish Festival, a fishing contest in which the fisherman with the largest catch wins the first prize. I have watched winners on TV display their catch and seen people scream, holding their head and saying, "pepper soup o!"

This is not Europe where people catch a fish, take a selfie with it, weigh and measure the fish, then throw it back into the water. Naija must eat the catch with gratitude for a life well-spent by the fish, which is always survived by numerous descendants (guaranteeing tomorrow's pepper soup). The ladies are not exempt, but they do not talk much. On seeing the large fish, they just remember their sharp knives and start humming their cooking tune (Naija ladies cook singing).

Mention must be made of paranoia which is a national past time. Yes, Naija United FC players (eleven on the pitch and two hundred million on the bench) love to fear things ranging from armed robbers and kidnappers to death by medically-unexplained ailments. The fear of hunger, however, is number one. So, just like all roads lead to Rome in bygone days, we find that, in contemporary Naija, all roads — good or bad — lead to food. With two hundred million palates and over thirty million farmers, Naija is the food capital of Africa.

We forgive the founding fathers of this great Food Club for erroneously trying to unite the nation behind a green-white-green flag and national anthem and then, lately, have sprang a national pledge on us all. It didn't work. They could have asked Moses who gave the Ten Commandments to the Israelites in the desert and saw the poor engagement with divine ordinances compared to the total compliance when manna from heaven arrived. They should have just used the everlasting slogan that never fails: *Food is ready*.

A MENU OF WASTE

NAIJA IS A COUNTRY WITH AN A LA CARTE menu that has waste as an essential ingredient of most meals. *Waste not want not* is quoted by the majority but heeded by a tiny minority. Everything is up for wastage: lives, destinies, natural resources, human potential, talents, geographical areas of outstanding natural beauty, good fortune, and all manners of opportunities.

When a culture of wastage exists for many years, food of course will get wasted.

The time spent in Lagos traffic listening to radio programmes full of adverts of "Promo! Promo!" is worse than a prison sentence (in some European prisons). Two to four hours a day for five days in the week means the tally at the end of the year is enough time to achieve a Diploma in Time Management from the local university.

Only the well-to-do can be accused of wastage. You need to have your cup running over to really indulge in the extravagant expending of valuable resources. Poverty usually follows when people with great harvests stay indoors while their crops rot on the trees. Hunger comes and loans are needed to import food from nations that do not have waste written into their national mission statement.

The irony of waste is that those deep in this culture feel special. Only the rich can waste after all, and the poor gaze in amazement when confronted with people pouring expensive bottles of wine on each other's heads. Nature, on the other hand, never wastes anything. The lions hunt down the antelope then eat until they are full then go away. Next comes the vultures to clear up the leftovers. They leave, and the bacteria do their job. Dust indeed returns to dust. The antelope vanishes without a trace, but some of its remains fertilise the soil for the next generation of plants.

Nigeria is a land where a seed thrown out of the window takes root and grows. The sunshine and rain are constant, yet people are hungry, and food is imported. Up to thirty percent of Nigeria's farm harvest is reported to rot away as transportation and refrigeration of food products are not at the level you would expect from a country with about thirty million farmers and two hundred million mouths to feed. The only food well-preserved is breast milk for the babies, and that is because the government is not involved in breast activities. If the Nigerian factor could affect breasts, then babies will starve due to the *not-on-sit* response that will answer the hungry lips requesting for a juicy nipple.

So many agricultural science departments dot the academic landscape of Nigeria, but these talents waste. They teach and set examinations for students, but they all eat imported rice. A harvest of classroom agricultural theories and no opportunities for practical action mean that the hunger continues. It must be frustrating to have the best agricultural mind in Africa and be born a Nigerian. Talent dey waste! Food processing is in its infancy because importation is how the big boys who control agricultural policies make their money.

I had my formative years in the early seventies oil boom in Lagos. I had no regard for food as a resource. Perhaps I was too young or the society was increasing in affluence daily. We were taught about cash crops in Primary school, groundnut pyramids, cocoa, palm oil, and cotton. There were maps of Nigeria with pictures of various crops dotted on different parts of the country. We were exporter of cash crops (and the foolish importers of chocolate and groundnut oil).

Unfortunately, those days are long gone with the waste.

People generally will waste most of what they get. That is why looking too closely at our lives might cause more depression than lessons learnt. Give a man a large sum, and he goes to the best restaurant, eats, and drinks all he can. Then, he goes home to vomit all. He wakes up to Panadol for his headache and repeats the cycle until the money is gone. The best managers of resources (on paper) are those who have lost everything. They desire with passion, tear another chance, and promise themselves how well they would look after their next opportunity. That second chance proves elusive in most instances. When they start to advice the *up and coming wasters about* the merits of making good use of every opportunity, the young guns call them *jealous have-beens*. It is a shame that the best placed instructors of how to avoid wastage are usually unattractive wasted souls who speak the truth mixed with a tinge of halitosis. Nobody listens to them.

I was wasteful with food as a child. A plate was seen as an arduous task put in front of us sometimes. Snacking on the garri that stood in a large plastic container in the corner of the kitchen was great. Drinking garri with ice cubes, sugar, and peak milk, you ate to your satisfaction and threw the rest in the bin.

Rice was eaten halfway and thrown in the bin. Eba, yams — the list is endless. Bin it when no one was looking. Bournvita, sugar, and peak milk finished and were replaced without inquisition. The 70s had milk and honey flowing in the streets of Surulere. But once we turned the corner and entered the 80s, my wasting career was over. I finished every grain on every plate and usually wanted more like the proverbial Oliver Twist. Worse was to come. Beans afflicted with weevils that would have been thrown away in the 70s were eaten in the 80s. Those like us who could not stand the look of dead and cooked insects in our plates looked forward as we ate avoiding eye contact with the insects destined for our stomachs. It was a price we all paid for being Nigerians in a country that had wasted the 60s and 70s. The opportunity to embrace newer methods of agriculture was wasted, and importation was the new cash cow.

The 80s saw the introduction of padlocks to domestic cupboards as access to beverages were now restricted. Children no longer walked to the fridges to eat and drink what they saw and fancied. An application process now came into force for children wanting to eat between their meals.

Unfortunately, the hunger continues for many. Someone once told me that if none of Nigeria's harvest rots, we have enough food for everyone even at today's production levels.

Let there be light!

ROMANTIC PLATES

WHEN A NAIJA MAN MEETS A NAIJA GIRL AND likes what he sees, they head to the eating house. That first date holds the destiny of their village people at the crossroads. Who will be in-law-to-who is determined by how the Naija girl responds to the long list of expensive items on the menu.

If she checks the prices and hisses, then comments on how she could cook soup that will last the week for the price being charged for the starters, the Naija boy makes a hasty retreat to the toilets. There he rings Mama to tell her he has found wife *material*. The first date is a two-way interview after all. Sitting face to face and looking into each other's eyes while soft lights and music caress the senses the way the gentle waves stroke the beach at Kamp Ikare resort, questions are asked and answered in a most unobtrusive way.

Naija girl knows she likes him, but she wants to see how he eats. She expects some form of irritation, and by sitting face to face, she is able to gauge if it is an irritation she could cope with till death does them part (or she has to resort to murder). At a given age, it is too late to change sucking and slurping sound effects when eating, so anybody wey no soji well will be hit with something. Eat *anyhow,* and there will be no next date. Eating together is what romance is all about, and marriage is the continuation of that eating together, long into the sunset when all romance is lost. The kitchen must be operational even if things are dead in the bedroom and the two parties are only *together for the children's sake.* Human beings can live without sex, but stop the food and see the real war start.

If two people cannot bear to watch each other eat, then the relationship crashes at take-off. Eating is natural and pleasurable, but it can be disgusting. Peeping through the lips to view masticated food is a view no one enjoys. It has similarities to peeping into a washing machine in full flow, but it is a hundred times more disgusting. I have never seen anyone smile with a mouth full of chewed up dodo and get photographed for social media. People sit there waiting, telling jokes trying to catch their date off guard, then boom! They catch a glimpse of the ugly slimy mess all over the tongue of their date. Once this is seen and the affection remains, then true love is possible.

Movie dates are a complete waste of time and the

Naija ladies know that any Naija man who suggests this as a first date is not serious about anything long-term. Eating popcorn while sitting side by side in darkness in an environment where no talking happens affords no real screening opportunity. There is no way of knowing if the date eats popcorn like a pig or a starving crazed shark. Noises they may make could be mistaken for movie sound effects.

After the plates have been cleared away, some people love to have deserts. Greedy people show themselves off at this stage by displaying oil-well kind of depth and width in their stomachs. The wine bibbers who finish a bottle and ask for another are noted. People who cannot stand gluttony make their minds up that this will be the last date.

The mouth is a window to the soul, but the soul lives in a fortified castle surrounded by a moat filled with water in which crocodiles swim. Food means the draw bridge needs to be let down for the food and drink to go in. Once the gates are opened to incoming traffic, out bound traffic can start to flow, especially when aided by wine. Information flows and key points are noted for investigation at a later date.

Wedding ceremonies emphasise the mutual feeding that is expected in Naija marriages. The cutting of the wedding cake is symbolic of how both partners' wealth will be joined into one big cake to be eaten by both parties. Then the family and friends will eat the cake too. Some men have signed up to the feeding of entire villages without knowing when they said *I do*.

The romance sometimes wanes with time, and special soups get to be mundane. Some sections of the Naija population literally spice up their marriages by adding spices to the food they cook. These are not the usual maggi cube type of spices. These are herbs you acquire by being taken to one *Baba* in the village. There is usually a wide range of *Apps* available such as only-eyes-for-you application, see-other-women-as-men software, and the dreaded native firewall that is guaranteed to make any girlfriend run mad after lovemaking with your husband. All these spices are added into the food.

Unfortunately, these same *Babas* sell to both camps. So when the man eats in his girlfriend's house, she adds spices to his food such as the give-me-more-money-than-you-give-your-wife juju and the all-eyes-on-the-side-chick juju (to the exclusion of other side chicks). In the end, the poor man's stomach becomes a war zone where various jujus and Apps battle it out for supremacy.

Should the man be polygamous (each wife would

have her own Baba, Imam or Pastor) and since he has more than three side chicks, he gets the services of his own *Baba to* neutralise every single plate of food he has to eat. This is usually with the kill-all juju malware spices in every food or drink App.

But Nigeria being what it is, double agents exit in the romance juju spices industry. Things get very complicated when eating out in establishments that have jazz put in the food by the restaurant owners to cause customers to return. Adding romance juju to such food really causes problems in the stomach.

Some Naija girls who have made up their minds about guys also invite them over to their homes for lunch. This is a way to display good housekeeping skills. The guy likes what he sees in a staged environment, and it is easier to add juju spices to his plate at home than in a restaurant.

As long as Naija boys and girls exist, there will be romantic plates of food shared.

WHAT NAIJAZ EAT

"Where shall we meet again? In the thunder lightning or in the rain?" asked the British delegate as the diaries were brought out. The Naija contingent to the conference looked on with barely concealed disdain.

"For what? You and who in lightning? Do I look like Sango's girlfriend? Please, it is this same Buka, same time next week abeg." The British murmured among themselves about how much "those Nigerians love their food" on the flight back home and with good reason.

The almost two hundred million Nigerians featured on the Worldometer website must be eating a lot of things to have that *live* number going up every fifteen seconds. With about two hundred and fifty tribes in Nigeria, with each boasting of its own cuisine, there is such a wide variety of foods to go through and not every Tom, Dick and Garri can be mentioned.

Every area of Nigeria has staple foods. The staples

can be divided roughly into the dough-like meals (also called swallows or solids) that are eaten with soups and the *others* – rice, bread, beans, plantains, and yams.

Beef, chicken, and fish are quite popular. Game and snails are favoured by some, but with the recent spate of Lassa fever infections (first described in Lassa Town, Nigeria in 1969 when the virus killed two missionary nurses), the demand for *bush meat* or *grass cutter* is on the wane.

The Swallows

Cassava-derived meals like akpu (fermented cassava), starch, lafun (cassava flour), and garri.

Yam-derived meals like amala (yam flour) and pounded yam.

Meals made from grains like tuwo dawa (guinea corn flour), tuwo massara (maize flour), and tuwo shinkafa (boiled rice).

Durum wheat-based pastes – semovita and semolina otherwise called *semo*.

Plantain-derived meals: plantain flour paste or *fufu*.

Cocoyam meal: ebiripo

The big combo: pounded yam, cocoyam and plantain all blended into one, (an Okrika/Ijaw swallow)

The Soups

Certain soups are well-loved in different parts of the country. Pepper soups and the tomato stew cut across most state boundaries and have become national dishes, but most soups just like the different languages tend to be concentrated in geo-nutritional zones.

The North

Miyan kuka (baobab leaves soup), muyina taushe (pumpkin soup) miyan zogale (zogale vegetable), and miya karkashi.

Middle belt

Soya bean chicken soup

The West

Ewedu soup

Niger Delta (South south)

Owo soup and banga soup

South East

Ofe nsala, afang, and edikang ikong soups

Due to the strong emotions that foods stir up as a result of their closeness to people's sense of identity, myths are bound to spring up around some certain foods which add a degree of mystery to them.

Santana/ Apku/Loi-loi

This meal is made from fermented cassava dough and has the power to make your visitors and neighbours ask if *una kill persin here as dead bodi dey smell?* This akpu preparation is a bit like child birth. When the baby arrives, the joy takes over. This meal is eaten with a soup of choice and is famed to have Duracell battery-like powers that make the body work for twelve hours without a break and with no sign of fatigue. Hence, its popular name of six to six (6am–6pm staying power).

A favourite among Igbos in South Eastern Nigeria, it sometimes plays second fiddle to pounded yam which is made from the king of crops — yam.

Miyam Kuka

This soup is quite popular up North and best eaten with tuwo made from the leaves of the most iconic tree on the planet, the baobab tree also called the tree of life. This is a meal that satisfies by reaching parts of the body and soul that other soups do not reach (allegedly).

The oldest trees in Africa are Baobab trees, and that adds an esoteric property to the leaves.

Edikang Ikong

This soup that is cooked by the Efik and Ibibio

people of the South Eastern part of Nigeria has an aura about it. People say that if a lady from that part of the country cooks this meal for a man, he loses his head and falls madly in love with her. It could just be that with so much variety in one pot, a man is sure to have all his gastronomic desires met (my theory). The soup is more congested than a packed molue and contains water leaves, goat meat, beef, dried fish, snail, stock fish, cow skin, palm oil, periwinkles, and crayfish. Enough to make the poor chap think, "I don't get this at home, but why? I need a change of address."

Ukodo

At the risk of being labelled as biased, I would simply say that Ukodo cooked by the right person in the right pot with the right yams and dried fish can reset your destiny. This meal is popular among the Urhobos of the Niger Delta.

Amala

For the Yorubas who inhabit the south western part of Nigeria, it might be safe to say that their world revolves around amala. Made from yam flour, it has the ability to make well-dressed people throw caution to the wind and risk stains on expensive white fabric. Having observed from close quarters, I am beginning to think that amala and that gbegiri soup has some mind-altering capabilities. It gives the eater an Amala worldview. Phrases like, *best thing since sliced bread* makes amala aficionados laugh inwards. They *know* that Amala is the best thing since the records of the best things in Nigeria began and that Amala is the only Titan that exists on the plates of Nigeria. The NASS, Native American tribe has a mythological giant called Amala who suspends the whole world on a stick. The day he tires and drops the stick, the world ends. For some in Nigeria, the world will surely end the day you tell them that the wooden spatula would stir the yam flour no more.

Miscellaneous

Jollof rice, moin-moin, ngwo ngwo (assorted meat in a soup), isiewu (goat head soup), coconut rice, achicha (dried cocoyam pottage), miya kubewa, abacha (salad from eastern Nigeria and no relative of the former military dictator), and gwaten doya (yam pottage) all keep the Nigerian stomachs happily engaged.

I must end with this; at every mealtime, an increasing number of Nigerians have been having a dish called *no meal*. This is due to poverty, and things need to change. Apart from people who are fasting or trying to lose weight, everyone else has a fundamental human right to eat something at every meal time. Abi I lie?

DELICIOUS TABOOS

I GREW UP KNOWING THAT MY DAD NEVER ate fried plantain. This was ironically my favourite food, so it became a case of one man's food taboo is another man's delicious taboo. He also didn't eat garri but stuck to only semovita aka *semo* with vegetable soup as his primary *swallow*.

I never heard people talk of food allergies or food intolerances when I was growing up. It was just "I dey forbid snail" or "for my place, pregnant women dey forbid grass cutter and palm wine." Naturally, we all have our preferences and while some like it hot, others like it cold.

In the 70s, there was always a superstitious slant that coloured people's food aversions. Many of these were not logical in any way. Ancestral spirits demanded libations of gin daily, however, forbade the villagers from eating cocoyams when the moon was out.

"Eggs will make a child steal."

"Congo meat (snails) will make a child's brain sluggish and cause the child to drool and sleep in class."

My dad ate bananas but not dodo (fried plantain). We didn't wonder why. We were too busy rejoicing that he would not reduce our rations. It was sometimes a jungle situation on the dinner table with adults at war with kids for life-giving foods. The most complex of all food beliefs was seen in the consumption of the head and eyes of a fish. This was linked to poor academic attainment, but parents never stopped you from eating the said fish head. They just teased you as you ate it. Now does the consumption of fish head really suppress intellectual development or do the people with low intelligence possess a gene that creates a great desire for the consumption of the head of fish?

Second bass jare!

Nowhere does food show its importance than in the one thousand days that mark the moment of conception to when the child turns two years of age. Maternal nutrition is important to the intrauterine development of the foetus, and this sensitive time is not when to avoid important foods on account of traditional taboos, yet it happens. For fear of having babies that are too big to be delivered naturally, uninformed would-be mothers avoid various foods to the detriment of their unborn children. They think they are avoiding Caesarean sections by intentionally eating less in pregnancy. After delivery, certain foods are denied to babies who are in a season of rapid growth and development. Protein is denied to kids while the male head of the house gets the biggest chicken. It is about time the children are viewed as the big fish in the pond at the dinner table and not their fathers. That Naija maxim, *"man muss wack"* needs to be transformed to the more appropriate: *child must wack.*

Second bass jare!

Food prejudices sometimes make sense. Vicious-looking animals truly should be avoided from entry into the kitchen. Bats, snakes, wolves, and spiders look mean and could do damage in the stomach. The ugly ones like vultures, hyenas, and crocodiles can stay far away from any human plate. These bad animals that can kill a man must not be eaten by a man for even in death, these bad boys retain their killer instincts. The animals with human traits, no matter how little the traits are expressed, should be taken as friends and not potential main courses. Dolphins, primates, elephants, cats, and dogs can share the planet with us human beings and be allowed to eat, not be eaten.

Alcohol is forbidden in pregnancy in some Naija communities, and that is excellent. Fetal alcohol spectrum disorders can lead to babies having hyperactive behaviours, poor memory, and poor language skills. Miscarriages and stillbirth rates increase when pregnant women drink alcohol.

Honey and sweets in pregnancy and in young children have their merits, but the rumour that these sweet foods cause worm infestations in the gut is a wonder. People just make up stories by linking unrelated events together. Conjectural principles are used in various Naija cultural settings when the pathophysiology of some diseases are not known.

Sometimes, admittance into various clubs and cults come with stipulation of foods to avoid (allegedly). There are royal fathers who are not allowed to eat certain foods or have their food cooked by women. Intriguing stories abound which are shared behind closed doors but never in public as everyone fears the royal fathers. The third Alaafin of Oyo was Sango (Thor to those who watch Marvel films), and he was famed for striking people with lightening. Upon his death and deification, his worshipers were forbidden from eating cowpeas.

They offer Amala as a sacred food to Sango, and they are allowed to eat amala in their downtime.

There are other religious groups that have food restrictions imposed on worshippers. Muslims do not eat pork while members of the Roman Catholic Church do not eat meat on Good Friday, but rather can eat fish. Everyone has their food fads. No one is exempt. When people invite you over for lunch, they ask about food allergies which is another way of asking you "if you dey forbid anything for una village." The spectrum of foods I eat is quite narrow.

People are creatures of habit and when in the supermarket, buy the exact same products and leave. Those who attend the traditional markets in Naija do not just stick to the same products but refuse to buy it from anyone else but Iya so and so. In social gatherings, many actually think their food fads make good conversation topics. They start listing restaurants they have been to that the ogbono did not agree with them (for some reason, Naija stomachs argue with foods). Now when this disagreement is between mother and food, she ropes her kids into the fight and she warns them against fraternising with the said food. Since she does the cooking, and wields the power, the child might be deprived of catfish which is now on the forbid list.

Second bass jare!

The Naija Food Philosopher has his own strict requirements for fine dining. The food must be dead, cooked, and spiced appropriately. None of those stews that consist of a thousand hot chilli peppers with two thin slices of onions and an eighth of a Maggi cube (awon Ondo girls, I hail o!). I only eat cooked meat derived from kind-faced animals—lamb and cows. Goats might be considered on alternate leap years. To that, there is no added sugar or sugary drinks of any kind, and I most definitely eat no street food or roadside sachet water in Naija. Some might feel that I am putting my nose up at their habits when I say, "no Buka for me," but they have not read any microbiology or public health books like the Philosopher.

To keep the body typhoid-free is a task that must be done

If you know, you know.

Then there is the no beer, no spirits, no coffee, no energy drinks and no tea rule. Reptiles and fowls of the air are forbidden. I am happy with chicken breast, thighs, and legs. No claws, heads, and bum bum. These are the taboos of mine. While on the matter, why do all Naija love songs serenade ladies with *chop my money?* What about saying, "The children we would have would chop my money." Or is giving eja nla to children a taboo matter again? Na the matter of poor food security for Naija children in the first one thousand days we dey judge since.

Second bass jare!

THE EASIEST NAIJA MEALS TO MAKE

Eating for some Naija people is more of an Eliud Kipchoge experience rather than a Usain Bolt one. These people are able to get that light bulb moment of approaching hunger and yet sit through the lengthy food preparation process deriving comfort and hope from the aroma of cooking that fills the air. They are the kind of people who would have been stars of the 1970 Stanford marsh mellow test where a treat was placed in front of a child with the promise of a second treat in fifteen minutes if they are able to sit there looking at the first treat (enduring temptation) without eating it. That means the first treat yielded a hundred percent return on investment if not eaten. The investment is delayed gratification.

Follow up studies showed that the children willing to invest in delayed gratification as a lifestyle did better in life. These Naija people with delayed gratification as the main agenda in their life have a motto: *soup wey sweet, na moni kill am,* meaning that the venison you see all spiced up in the ogbono arrived via first class and expensive transportation. Their adopted anthem is *Wait for me* by Onyeka Onwenu featuring King Sunny Ade. A song about delayed gratification for another kind of food.

But there is the other half of Naijaz who are more Usain Bolt than Eliud Kipchoge. They just cannot wait and when the starting gun signalling the arrival of hunger sounds in their brain, they must rush food through the lips in under ten seconds. Immediate gratification is the name of the game. Their motto is, *a bird in hand is worth twenty in the bush* while their anthem goes thus:

I cannot kill myself; allow me to flex.

Demand is the mother of all supply in the land of capitalism, so the market caters for the immediate gratification subset of Nigeria's population by making easy-to-make foods available.

Indomie instant noodles is the king of easy-to-make meals. Made by an Indonesian company, they have cornered the market in Nigeria following their arrival. Pre-packed food needing a bit of cooking in water strikes a chord with those who want the instant gratification that comes from a sudden freedom from hunger. With various flavours to suit every palate, it is obvious why this product is so successful. The absence of time-consuming steps like peeling onions and chopping peppers or the peeling of yams and plantain means the meal is ready in a few minutes with minimum wash up time after the meal. Freedom from effort is very attractive to people. There is also less risk of injury and pain while making instant noodles. Most knife cuts in the kitchen occur when slicing through beef or peeling potatoes.

Easy-to-make foods need to be easy on the pocket. While the other half might say *soup wey sweet na moni kill am*, the instant chefs will say *food wey quick, na indomie kill am*. Indomie is relatively cheap and easily affordable. While a piece of yam bought a few weeks ago will rot away and that nice ogbono soup will be assassinated by NEPA in a fridge turned oven, instant noodles seemingly live forever in their packaging reinforced by preservatives.

The absence of round the clock electricity means even nature's snacks such as fruits, which can be had while waiting for the main meals to be ready, cannot be stored. Oranges, bananas, pineapples, and mangoes are no match for the tropical heat. Refrigeration and tropical heat go together in today's world, but Naija appears to be on an entirely different planet.

Faster than noodles, the rapid-response food of all time is soaking garri. Garium sulphate as it is affectionately called just needs water poured in, and the food drink of champions is ready. Groundnuts and sugar are optional and milk is extravagant. Ice cubes on garri (garium on the rocks) is just good old showing off that you have light (or gen).

For some, drinking garri is a by-word for suffering and hardship, but *smoking garri* has been saving and delivering souls since Nigeria began.

Bread is another lifesaver, and it can be grabbed in a fit of hunger and molested while waiting for the butter to arrive. Tinned sardines, stew, or eggs go well with bread.

Among the instant gratification subset, some have long ago given up on making it home when hunger strikes. This is not entirely their fault because sometimes people are hungry, angry, and hot on the congested roads and further burdened with a full bladder. The thought of going home to visit the kitchen is not acceptable to them. The market has responded with fast food outlets everywhere. Food so speedy, it gets to you before the starting gun, signaling the start of hunger, has its trigger pulled.

"Gala! Gala! Gala!" they chant at your window while you are stuck in traffic, promising hunger palliation. Like one hypnotised, you buy and promptly divide into twice to see if you have more pastry roll than sausage roll. Biscuits, sweets, soft drinks, and various fruits are all for sale in Lagos traffic.

The roads are dotted with MamaPuts — local cafes serving hot food out of cramped premises that spill out to the pavement. Maishai are the Lagos version of Costa, Starbucks, and McDonalds all rolled into one providing breakfast for people on the go. The Maishai are predominantly Northerners who make tea, coffee, and sandwiches at neck-breaking speed for commuters. They offer some showbiz by pouring hot tea from a right hand cup held sky high into the left hand cup held as low as possible as they mix the tea. They are all like the Tom Cruise character, Flanagan, in the 1988 movie Cocktail (well, not exactly like Tom Cruise).

There are hawkers who walk the street, carrying their wares, but it may be impossible to time one's instant hunger with their arrival. Those who drive and can plan their routes take advantage of the fast food and traditional restaurants such as Mr Biggs, Chicken Republic, Tastie Chicken, Tantaliser, and the Kilimanjaro restaurant chain.

Some restaurants will do takeaway orders and deliver, but the instant gratification crew will still make their telephone orders and then walk over to the corner of the street to buy boli (roasted plantain) and fish to hold belle as they hum Bob Marley's *Waiting in vain*.

THE FOOD CABALS

Like a nation under a trance, Naijaz present themselves with healthy appetites and sit with the steering spoon gazing longingly as a mist of aroma rises out of their hot plates of food. There is usually no thought of how this food made its journey over land, sea and air to arrive on the ceramic altar. Like Naijaz say, *if you know, you know,* but, unfortunately, no one appears to know or even care to know about the food cabals.

It is no different from the epic movies. People ignore the credits and walk away at the end of the movie. They recall the star actors but don't care much about the behind-the-scenes cabals that ignite the entertainment industry away from prying eyes.

The Mother of all the food cabals in Naija is of course *awon mummy*. The sweet mother ladies that feed the nation. They determine the salt consumption of the nation as well as the blood cholesterol levels of everyone as they run our forty million kitchens, cooking up storms, floods, and poodles. The men just sit and eat what is put in front of them. Even professional male chefs have been known never to cook at home. Millions of pot bellies doted around the country owe their calabash body shape to awon mummy. With catch phrases like, "finish that food o," they ensure the country is well-fed and, in some isolated cases, overfed. The chances of catching gastroenterological diseases are also in the hands of awon mummy and wifey. In Nigeria, only two people tell you, "I will kill you," and you know you are dead. They are God and wife. *If you know you know.*

The ideal cabal are those whose very existence is called into question. These are the ones who claim they are only providing a service with clean hands and a clear conscience, but we know they have all sworn allegiance to a secret cult. Case in point are the Naija wedding reception ushers. In the words of Otunba Churchill: "Never in the field of Naija party animosity has so much bile been bestowed by so few on so many." Everybody appears to hate the wedding ushers, and there are a thousand conspiracy theories in circulation about them.

Receptions always run late and guests are hot, hungry, and angry. There lies the power of the slim ladies prancing around with trays of snacks, walking past tables of salivating grown-ups. Challenge them as they go and you hear, "She is coming to serve your table." She speeds off without saying who the *she is*.

Discrimination is on various levels. The ushers serve those they know well. At other times, some serve only those wearing their own Aso Ebi, acting on *orders from above*, aka senior cabal. Soft drinks are usually democratised and free for all, but meat and party souvenirs are strictly on a who-know-man basis. The only buck to this trend is if you are a very big man or if you are a white man. Even ushers love the rich and the foreigners (those from Gabon and Ghana should not hold their breath as ECOWAS and Naijaz get the same treatment). Once tortured by these receptions, panic sets in. The guest fans himself furiously to hide the sweat as he fears that food may finish, and he will be doomed to a long drive home on an empty stomach. Ironically, toothpicks never finish.

The queens that hold the spoons like a royal sceptre in the area are the MamaPuts. Those who know, kiss the ring. When money is low and you order food that will not fill a toddler, she knowingly lets a few pieces of meat *accidentally fall* into your plate to cover your hunger and shame. If her son is Kunle, you must ask about Kunle and Papa Kunle every time you see her. She has the memory of an elephant and even bigger ears; nothing misses her. She seats majestically and controls the happiness of most drivers on the road each day with her spoon. Rumours abound as to what they put in their stew, but the Naija public really don't expect recipes to be published by a cabal.

Spirits and Sprites have their say on this food matter. The Urhobos worship Edjokpa, the god of palm trees for a bumper harvest. Things-fall-apart phenomena, however, raised its ugly head, and this god, set up as a one-man cabal, was last seen in Malaysia, hustling for foreign exchange as it felt unappreciated by both NIFOR (Nigerian Institute of Oil Palm Research, Ogogugbo, Benin City) and the many Urhobos whose libations fell short of ECOWAS' spiritual regulations. Needless to say, Edjokpa has worked wonders for the Malaysians who lead the world in palm oil production through its made-in-Nigeria Tenera oil palms.

On the libation matter, the evil forest cabals collect a certain libation tax on all harvests in Nigeria. Deeming the drops of palm wine poured out in libation to ancestors inadequate, they take libation tax at source. They cause thirty to fifty percent of everything harvested in Nigeria to rot. These evil spirits that waste our food supply, however, go unchallenged, and no one prays against the evil forest cabal. Many claim the harvests waste because there is a lack of adequate storage facilities, however, even though the existence of the evil forest cabal cannot be proven in a lab, *if you know, you know.*

Some churches do harvest thanksgiving services when the bumper harvest comes around (celebrating what was left over after the evil rotting process), and hopefully, they would move from just thanking God to attacking evil.

The other set of cabals are the multinationals. Most Naijaz buy products, tear the packaging, then consume. Few read the wordings on products to know who makes what they eat and what has been put inside. The end users, with the plate in front of them, do not even know what brands have gone into the meal preparation of the food he is thanking God for. Cabals like it this way. It is called anonymous hammering.

At the breakfast table, Naijaz seat with the Nestle cabal, makers of nido, milo, nescafe coffee, and carnation milk. Many have been drinking milo from birth and know nothing about Nestle. On leaving home with a belly full of Nestle products, the traffic stress quickly digests the stomach contents and the UAC Nigeria cabal is ready to serve you Gala sausage roll (since 1962) and perhaps some Fun Time Coconut Chips and Swan bottled water. Break time at work means it is off to Mr Biggs to bless the UAC pockets once again, and then it is back to work to tidy off the day's job paying tribute to Unilever via Lipton tea. Peak milk comes by way of Friesland Campina Wamco.

After work, it is down to the local *point and kill* for pepper soup and beer. Nestle smiles, collecting its tribute as Naijaz are not capable of cooking without adding Maggi cubes. As for the Brewery companies, they are a cabal as they buy all the sorghum to make beer. The drive home is punctuated by a stopover at a suya joint where beef and chicken lie side by side at high temperatures, sizzling in the dark. The Fulani herdsmen are a strong cabal who supply the beef here. Chicken comes from all over but the biggest poultry is Oatvana Farms in Okpe local government area, Delta State. This is the largest chicken campus in Nigeria, and they graduate students yearly with a hundred percent employment rate on plates across the country.

Soon, it is back to the traffic and the kids ring to say good night.

"Have you eaten?"

"Yes, daddy. Mummy made us Indomie!" they answer. That seems to be all his children ever eat he thinks but says nothing to avoid a war with awon mummy food cabal. Safer to just pay his daily tax to the

Dufil Prima Foods Company and let Indonesia and Singapore chop a bit of his salary.

By the time the Naija man gets home, he has the whole world in his stomach, and he has paid tribute to the cabals he knows not of as each one takes a few naira here and there. He knows not who he maketh rich daily.

The last cabals have no offices or state registration. We know they exist, and all Naijaz eat their products. These are the food smugglers. Your satisfaction and money are their delight. They are friends to everyone and have loyalty to no one. The police, customs officers, warehouse owners, retailers, and customers know who they are, but ironically, do not know who they are. *If you know, you know.*

Epilogue

Though not a cabal yet, the future belongs to the farmers on laptop, hoping to gift Naija with an agricultural-based digital industrialisation. Armed with drones, AI, robots, smart seeds, crowd funding skills, and the intellect to stop thirty to fifty percent of Nigeria's agricultural output rotting away, new guns are the future. They are the Agro-tech cabals.

VULTURE UNITED FC (FOOD CLUB) OF NAIJA

Scavengers provide an important Service, and as a 70s kid, I was a paid up member of this club.

As children of the oil boom Nigeria, there were leftovers to pack away and dispose of (in our stomachs) after every visitor had been entertained. That was how we knew the taste of every spirit and beer we were not allowed to drink. As soon as you turned the corner and escaped the prying eyes of those left in the sitting room, you turned the bottle or glass upside down and savoured a few drops—Guinness, Schnapps, Teachers Whiskey, White Horse, Dubonnet, Mateus Rose, Top Beer, Gulder, Star, and Heineken—we tasted all.

On one particular day, I was over zealous in my waiter-scavenger role, and I cleared a bottle of Fanta off the table with a forty percent residual. "I don hammer," I thought. As I lifted the curtains to leave the sitting room, her husband put the proverbial sand in my garri. "Wilson, she didn't finish it. Bring it back, let me help her." Wickedness! This was the same *Oliver Twist* uncle that ate his meat and went on to finish the wife's meat and bones.

Sometimes, parents will implore the visitors to eat, but we countered it with prayers that the spirit of satiety will fall on the visitors. Christmas was bonanza time. Visitors on multiple visits arrived with full stomachs, and we just knew that the served meat will not return to the pot as it has been classed as chop remain, and the scavengers would be called into action. It was a talent we had then—eating between meals at the drop of a hat and still looking thin. Rapacious children we were. Abi we had worms???

This great scavenger activity had to be done clandestinely for if caught, the punitive measures might spoil a promising weekend. With due reasons, drinking from the used beer glasses of visitors was a punishable offence. In those days, you had tag-along visitors who had been visiting the primary visitor and then decided to *escort* to your house. What if they had undiagnosed tuberculosis? Even in instances where the families were well-known, not all visitors received with pleasantries were really welcomed. Couples could be embraced as they walked through the door, but the host family knew mummy called *aunty* a witch.

The sweets she brought must be handed back to mummy, and her leftovers were deemed to be beneath even the family dog's level.

Leftovers are strange things. Many don't even fancy their own leftovers. A few men have this new-soup-everyday policy which looks like either an obsessional behaviour or the terms and conditions for joining a cult. While most people deem leftovers to be food that remains on a plate after the served food has been eaten, some hard-core people feel that anything cooked over two hours ago is a leftover and should not be eaten. "They obviously have too much money," some might think and rightly so. The other end of the spectrum are those Naijaz who believe that all food is everlasting. These are ones who would never read the *best before date*.

They work on the premise that *food no dey kill African man*. These are the ones who actually think they have the acidic stomachs of vultures. *Moderation in all things* is a worthy maxim to live by. The wisdom embedded here shows the centre of the spectrum to be okay.

For health reasons, one has to be careful whose food to continue eating after they have finished. Some irrigate their food with spittle during meals, and that is okay since the food and their microbes end up in their stomachs. Not really advisable for others to eat such. Romantic involvement, however, changes the rules. What are a few drops of saliva on steak among regular kissing partners?

Hardship has driven people to eat out of dustbins. That is hard to take no matter how clean the bins are. This happens all over the world, and, hopefully, this will end one day.

My vulture career, it appears, never stopped. I became a supervisor cum coach in the team by the time I was an A Level student in boarding house in FGC Kaduna. At mealtimes, food was divided according to how many table members we had. While we ate, eyes moved like that last scene in the Spaghetti western The Good, The Bad, and The Ugly. Eyes darting to the extra fish in the pots and the served plates of people who might be running late, too ill to come over to the dining hall or on home leave.

Some juniors might suggest that someone was not coming, but as the senior at the table, I looked at my watch, took in the information, and asked for everyone to keep eating. Supper was timed, and five minutes to the end of the meal, I gave the sign; it was *massacre time*. The excess food was eaten in a feeding frenzy as it was an abomination for fried fish to return to the kitchen as leftovers. It got ugly sometimes, but good was being done. Why throw away yams that would encourage rats that might bring Lassa fever along? Better the digested yams going down the toilet. The greed was bad though as some sat eating their portion and having fantasies of fellow students' plates.

Now in adulthood, I look around and think about life, and Naija is one big Savannah plain full of jackals, hyenas, and vultures. A ghastly car accident scene was once attended by first-aiders who were really self-aiders. They checked the pockets of the victims before checking for a pulse.

In the jungle, where the lion is king, there are no courts or murder trials. There are no burials. The survival of the fittest means one animal's loved one is another animal's lunch. The lion eats, and the leftovers are for the vultures, jackals, and hyenas. Then the ants come. That way, the savannah is not littered with disease-producing carrion.

Naijaz like to look at men on seats for we all know deep down that every chair is an electric chair waiting for *NEPA* to bring light. A seat at the table, however, provides an opportunity to eat until your time is up. Enemies will bribe *NEPA* to connect light to your chair, hence even atheist Naijaz pray for *a table prepared for me in the presence of my enemies.*

Monitoring spirits know a man's assets for they have the keen vision of vultures and have the wing span to soar majestically in ugly flight to survey a life. They have tongues to curse to death and beaks strong enough to pierce any hidden bank account enclosed in steel vaults. Their long necks are what we call long throat. *Chop alone, die alone* is the subtle threat Naija vultures give in jest, but the only punch line is a blade through the spleen.

My beloved game, football, comes to mind. To occupy a position on the field of play is akin to be majestically prancing around on the savannah. In the stadium, crowds watch and viewers at home monitor via satellites that encircle like vultures. That position is coveted strongly by someone else who has an agent, family members, and fans. The minute a wrong tackle sends the player down, the coach signals to his replacement to warm up, and many observers rejoice. There can be no vacuum in nature. One man's fall is another man's promotion.

That is the circle of life, and in every successful cycle, someone must do the good, the bad, and the ugly work.

Epilogue

I must acknowledge Nigerians worldwide who attend Naija celebrations with their personal *plastic containers* in true vulture-scavenger mode. This consistent work has ensured that not even a grain of party jollof rice has been thrown in the bin in the last seventy years. Weddings, birthdays, funerals, naming ceremonies, and even family gatherings during the festive seasons run in an eco-friendly waste-free manner because of you. Special thanks to those who were not really invited so turned up without their plastic containers but, through resourcefulness, grab a bin liner or aluminium foil and start scavenging. Shout out to all the legends that just carry the party pot of stew home and then text the celebrant for an address to return the pot to the next day.

Party organisers that actually make plastics containers for takeaways available to guests will all make heaven.

FOOD CHAIN PINNACLE

YOU CANNOT CLIMB THE TREE BEYOND THE highest leaf. Once at the top, if care is not taken the only way is down. The Naija people are surely at the top of the West African Food Chain. Being at the pinnacle means we have a right to kill everything that moves to satisfy the appetite. I grew up watching animals being killed—fish, crabs, chicken, turkeys, goats, and rams. There was one particular incident that has stayed with me.

A slim butcher was hired to kill a neighbour's ram, and we all gathered to watch the silencing of the bleating animal. The butcher put up a mini show. First, he opened up his small blanket on the floor to reveal various knives of different sizes. Then he began to sharpen them by striking them against each other and causing a few sparks to fly. The mumu ram seemed to be enjoying the spectacle as much as we were. A large pot of water had now been heated to boiling point in the corner of the compound using fire wood as fuel.

This was Circa 1974 Christmas season in Lagos. With deft movements, the butcher's understudy had the ram wrestled to the floor with both fore and hind legs tied. The butcher had made his selection. It was a long blade that slit the ram's throat. Blood poured forth, and the ram cried like someone who had been betrayed. The legs twitched, and the whole body went limp.

The next act was even more exciting. The butcher took off his shirt to reveal a Sahel savannah kind of chest and moved to tie a ligature around the neck of the animal. He then freed the right hind leg and made a cut in it at the ankle. He took a deep breath that saw his abdomen disappear and his chest ballooned up to three times its normal size, and then he fixed his mouth over the leg wound and blew into it with all his might. His eyes popped out as he blew air into the carcass and the veins on his neck and head became prominent like snakes. He continued blowing, with cheeks puffed out so big you thought they just might burst.

After a few minutes, the ram looked like a Michelin man that might take flight into the Lagos sky at any moment. It was then the butcher finished with a flourish. He took a breath so deep, air flowed in from the next street. He then exhaled with so much force that when he farted, people ducked like an armed robber had fired a rifle. His cheeks puffed up so much as he held the leg to his mouth that an astonished agbalaba shouted, "Dizzy Gillespie!" He then tied the ram's legs with a ligature above the wound to keep the air in. Next, his understudy poured the hot water on the ram's ballooned body as the butcher who had now changed knives began to shave the hair off the animal.

The adults had now started arguing who the greatest trumpeter in the nation was and how much the butcher's puffy cheeks and neck measured up to Dizzy G. We young ones left them with their boring conversation. We knew the butcher will carve up the animal, and we would get our dues as kings of the food chain.

Incidentally, it was a surgeon who taught me, in later years that air could leak into the tissues of human beings when their gullet ruptures causing the chest, neck, and face to swell like the Michelin man. This is called Surgical Emphysema.

The Naija Food Philosopher has never killed an animal for food before, and it is very unlikely to happen. The plants beckon me to a life of vegetarianism, but the king of the food chain does as he pleases. Some of my countrymen abuse their position at the summit of the food chain. They kill and eat reptiles and rodents. They need to take caution.

Even the egungu (masquerade) approaching the expressway is cautioned and pulled back for no one is invincible. Those with positions of authority must exercise restraint and responsibility.

There was a certain visit to a family friend that had me bewildered in childhood. It turned out that our hosts bred rabbits, and it was delightful to go on a tour to the cages. The animals looked cute, but while I saw the relatives of Bugs Bunny, my host confided in me that he saw meat floating in his stew when he looked at them.

It sounded like murder to me. Some animals have a personality. Same like dogs and cats. Still the crazy ones kill them for food.

BEANS IS BUSINESS

No FOOD EVER SPOKE TO THE NAIJA FOOD philosopher till late December 1985. It lasted for thirty minutes, but the words have lasted a lifetime. Since then, I have been around the world eating and drinking while meditating on my country's great culinary heritage. On planes, I have listened to rappers spit bars while I in turn munched bars of the good *stuff*. I had drank the stuff, chewed on it, nibbled at it, licked, and sucked it to great delight. I thought I knew chocolate until that night in 1985 when, as I drifted into sleep, I saw three little cocoa beans dressed in agbada and fila, bearing the tribal marks of an Ibadan man. Their leader asked me politely, "Do you know who I am?"

The question was not unfamiliar to a Naija boy. We all like to ask this question of our compatriots in Nigeria. We all desperately wish to be recognised like Amala. We love to be introduced as *an individual who needs no introduction.*

I looked closely and couldn't tell who he was. A shrivelled up agbalumo fruit or a bloated blackeyed bean? I looked into the eyes of the one who spoke and said, "I don't know you from Adam." He was upset. He looked at his two friends and made an eye signal to one of them who spoke up, "Do you know Kit Kat, Mars Bar or Bournvita?"

I nodded. "You want to eat?" I asked.

"We are their ancestors. We are the three cocoa beans of the West," he said and suddenly disappeared. I heard them humming even though they were now out of sight, "*I'm looking for my Johnny. Where is my Johnny?*" It was a song by Yemi Alade they were singing albeit years before its release. What followed next was like a download into my brain. I suddenly knew things I hadn't known before. I saw the past, present, and the future simultaneously. I saw Tetteh Quarshie of Ghana travel to Fernando Po and return with cocoa which he cultivated and later passed on to Nigeria where the Western part of the country took to cocoa cultivation like a fish to water. The money flowed in, and there was even a great building called Cocoa House.

I had never seen cocoa seeds before. Strange but true, despite living not too far from the farms. I was a student, not a farmer. I was a consumer, not a producer. A child of the oil boom, not one of the agrarian boom of the sixties.

I was asleep, but I tasted chocolate in my mouth as I saw visions of a million cocoa beans travelling in ships to Europe. The Naija Food Philosopher began to think in his sleep. Strange how food travelled out to Europe — in ships. They travelled with the purpose of making Cadbury great. Naija food in the stomach of Europeans!

If Cocoa could grow in England, who would have bothered transporting it across the sea? If sugar and tea could grow in London, who would import it? Why did people develop a taste for food their land could not produce? Well, good ships and big fat canons can get you anything your heart desires.

The great explorers Mungo Park and Henry Stanley who travelled to Africa. What did they eat throughout their respective stays? These great discoverers should have taken the natives to the River Niger and River Congo respectively, but the native guides took them there because the great Rivers can only know true greatness when a European discovers it for himself. Discover is a byword for exploiting the economic benefits that may accrue.

The African land was always portrayed as barbaric and primitive, but why did they keep on coming back?

It was business. Racism is business in disguise. That is the only means to secure food, minerals, and human labour for free or peanuts. The man who is higher seeks no permission but just grabs it. Superior ammunition makes men *higher human beings*. No one asks permission from a chicken before taking its egg, despite the chicken having great plans for the egg. The breakfast table needs to be furnished; end of story.

Still tasting chocolate on my tongue, I began to hum, "I'm looking for my Johnny" Suddenly, this white guy appears, wearing a glowing white agbada with a face covered in Ibadan tribal marks.

"I am Otunba Johnny Cadbury, the chocolatier number one. The founder of Cadbury which is stationed at Bourneville in Birmingham. No one can drink any alcohol in the area around my factory."

I didn't have to be told twice. I prostrated flat to greet the ancestor, the Quaker and creator of all things nice.

"Stand up you yeye boy. You Naija people are the owners of the cocoa na. We just ground it and sold it back to you." He then proceeded to lie down flat and prostrate before me. A whole agbalagba. I was in severe embarrassment. "Ancestor, please, stand up. I was brought up on Bournvita that your company made and sold to us after processing our cocoa."

Then I grew angry. This was what we called an Israelite journey. Cocoa in Ibadan travels to Lagos, boards a ship for London, travels by train to Birmingham, gets converted to Chocolates and Bournvita, the food drink of champions and then travels to London, boards a ship for Lagos, checks out at the Apapa wharf, and it is off to the warehouse.

Why didn't the cocoa just travel from Ibadan to a Surulere chocolate factory? And then we sell our own chocolate and Surulerevita to the British.

Otunba was reading my thoughts. "I don't mean to be rude, but you guys have the cocoa trees, and we have the sense," he said. At this point, I was livid and ready to slap an elder, but he disappeared.

I thought of all the chocolate drinks all over the world. What if we refused to sell our cocoa and just sold our Surulerevita and Surulere Chocolate Bars to the world? Imagine getting a cut from every chocolate ice cream going between lips. Now that would be something nice.

That is power — to own the chocolate of the world. It is, however, one thing to own the cocoa and another thing to have the military power to guard the cocoa. The powerful army will always come over to *explore and discover*. *Discover* is just a fancy word for noticing opportunities for financial gain and making sure that a good price is not requested for the product.

King Jaja of Opobo requested a good price for his palm oil, and years later, Ghaddafi suggested crude oil be traded with gold and not dollars. *No bi from my mouth you go hear wetin happen to Africans wey demand good price.*

Demanding a good price is akin to Oliver Twist asking for more. That means more beatings.

By the time I woke up, I was so angry. I just grabbed my bread and washed it down with Bournvita. Hunger destroyed the entire cocoa boycott I was planning in my sleep. The meal proved too delicious, and I was back in bed. I dozed off, and what happened next was astonishing. A carnival procession rode into town. I saw the three cocoa beans from the west dancing joyously with Otunba Johnny Cadbury who had his sons dancing on both sides. They were George and Richard Cadbury.

Out of nowhere danced in Tetteh Quarshie, wearing a kente cloth with gold thread running through its length. He stole the show. I was shocked that I knew their names. I asked the cocoa beans what they think they had achieved in their lifetime. "We have moved our next generation into Ivory Coast and led the world in cocoa production. That child labour problem breaks our hearts though." A great crowd clapped. I posed the question to everyone. Otunba Johnny said, "I founded a great brand and fought against child labour in Birmingham through my campaign to stop the use of children as chimney sweeps." Nore hands clapped.

I wanted to join in, so I blurted out loudly, "I have eaten chocolate sweets all my life. I have dental extractions to prove this." No one clapped for the Naija Food Philosopher. I felt like one of those people who came to the planet just to eat and do little. Amongst all these great men, one feels really unicellular. I so desperately wanted to wake up.

Otunba George Cadbury spoke next. "I founded the model village Bourneville. It was an excellent community for my staff at the time." The earth shook with applause. Tetteh Quarshie spoke next: "Charlie, I introduced cocoa to Ghana and Nigeria and look at what it has contributed to the economy of West Africa." The cocoa beans in their voluminous agbadas prostrated in respect. The Cadburys lifted their hands, clapping. I felt ashamed and wondered what I could say.

"I live in the city and regularly run the Birmingham half marathon for charity and when we run past Bournville, I always salute," I said. They all clapped hard. I was pleased. But trust Naija men not to let matter lie in peace.

Suddenly, we had a man pull up in a chocolate-coloured Rolls Royce. When he stepped out of the back seat, he was dripping with swag. The Ghana-Nigeria cat and mouse argument continues even in death. Everyone cheered as he drew close. It was James Labulo Davies, famed for introducing Cocoa agriculture to Nigeria. "Tetteh Quarshie, you were saying?" he said.

Tetteh Quarshe began to stammer, "Charlie, I introduced it to Ghana and maybe Nigeria, but it has been such a long time. My memory fails me."

"It does indeed. I am the original cocoa-master of Nigeria. Husband to Sarah who was Queen Victoria's god daughter. My sweet cocoa money still speaks even today in Bariga. Did I not finance the establishment of CMS Grammar School, Lagos? Incidentally, it was over hot cups of cocoa that I made the funds available to Reverend Thomas Babington Macaulay."

I was so vexed to find myself awake. I had so many questions for the cocoa-master. I wanted more time in their world. Perhaps, I am just an Oliver Twist.

I wonder when we would produce our own indigenous Cadbury. When? I read about one lady called Femi Oyedipe who might be Naija's chocolate messiah. Cross River State in south eastern Nigeria has built a cocoa-processing plant. The future is chocolate.

GREAT POTS OF AFRICA

THE POTS THAT FED THE CONTINENT SINCE the start of the ages are now resting in peace. Clay pots now one with Mother Earth. They lie side by side in the dust next to the multitudes that cooked out of them, stored palm wine in them, and balanced them on their heads during that long journey back from the stream. Like the earth, round and made for just one burner, the pots sat majestically in stillness and dignity on fire wood flames. From afar, the inner core could never be seen, but move close and fumes erupt from the mouth of the pot. Like delightful sweet volcanoes, you smelt the ameidi soup and without words being spoken, you knew which kind of soup mama was cooking.

A million billion sliced yams have been cooked in you great pots of Africa. A million forgetful young wives have left you on the fire only to remember their *dinner in progress* when the soup has been burnt to ashes. You eavesdrop on all the stories, you great pots

301

of timelessness. For our mothers never cooked in silence. They taught their daughters and warned their friends as they stirred the pepper soup. You heard about who to marry and who not to visit. The pot heard intimate secrets, but never told anyone what it had seen; that is all pots except the shrine pots that speak to the voodoo priests at full moon.

The village potters had mystical hands that sweated in the tropical heat. Shrine pots, ornamental pots for the palace, decorative pieces for the brides and mothers, they were all formed from the clay mined in the east side of the village. Once formed and dried, they gathered all the pots for a baptism of fire. There was a ferocious glazing process with a fire so intense that the pots changed their disposition and were sure to stop leaking soups or tales.

It was these ancient pots that entertained visiting Europeans who came to trade. The hospitality was divine, but the visitors had eyes on the serving dishes and handcrafted pottery. Eyes that went home to dream of the artistic masterpieces they had seen. They returned for a second visit, repaying hospitality with hostility. Guns, whips, and the looting of pots to distant lands followed. These are the living-dead pieces in foreign lands who wish to be buried in Africa. They lie in state perpetually in museums around the world, and their vagabond spirits pine for home. The pots earnestly wish to be buried next to the people who drank out of them. But no, they are on display to the children of their abductors behind glass walls. Emptied of the soups they once knew and denied any fire on their bottom, these lonely pots strike a forlorn figure, looking sideways at statutes of Kings and Obas who ate out of them centuries before civilised people came visiting. *When will I see my home?*

From Botswana to Nigeria and from Accra's Ghana to Senegal's Dakar, potters have sculpted masterpieces for nobility and common men. Terra cotta, ceramics, and the ubiquitous clay pots all tell a story without speaking a word. Pots, round and smooth like the African queens that cooked with them, beer pots so large and brown like the bellies of the men who drank from them, they all rest in peace now. The potbellied men and the pot-bottomed women dwelling in harmony with their pots. Resting in the earth till their peace is shattered once again by the invaders, the archaeologists who come to snoop for artefacts to take away to distant museums. The pots which the original invaders did not have time to take away, well, the second invaders will collect all that remains.

So many meals have been cooked and served in

Africa. With love and care, fresh food was presented in pots. Yet it wasn't all about the cooking. AD 419 saw a native scientific breakthrough when a lady who walked on her head on market days poured water in a pot and starting seeing moving images on her native plasma screen. She called a man and just like she was using a TV remote control, there was a channel change — his face appeared. She stuck a broom through his chest, and blood filled the pot until his image disappeared. He was buried shortly after, and that was how the internet was conceived — in the pots of Africa.

It was customary for communities to eat from the same pot. On big feast days, resources were pooled and food was prepared centrally in giant pots. In Morocco, they have the tagine pot that contained the tagine food. The food and the earthenware pot shared the same name. Their bellies should have been called tagine. This is unity and serves up a cohesive society for the nation that eats from the same pot stays together.

AD 419 was a great year in the territory now named Nigeria. Dafe, the astronomer who dwelt in what is present day Ughelli taught his students that the earth was a pot in motion around the great Sun whose heat was maintained by Oghene's everlasting firewood.

And this was why the earth always produced delicious things. There were other planets in this solar system, each a pot in its own right. He named each planet after his Urhobo soups but soon the planets were renamed by Europeans after Greek and Roman gods. Herein is the proof that the one holding the biggest gun always gets to name both planets and countries. Might is right, and military and naval superiority have always decided who grabbed the pot and writes the history.

The great Dafe was years ahead of his time. While sections of the world were talking about the earth being flat, his ancestors had taught him that it was round. Mama Africa with her two huge ovaries studded with gold produced the children in her womb, and Papa Africa visited, dragging along with him two pots of sperm cells swimming in crude oil and diamonds. Pots of treasures mixed with wombs that incubated greatness on the most fertile part of the planet brought forth an explosion of wealth and fortune. Dafe had said that this much wealth and flamboyance would attract attention, but no one heeded the astronomer.

Europe was attracted to the wealth; they came for all the best pots and spots. It wasn't enough for them. They came back to take away the people that made the pots so beautifully. Mama and Papa Africa were exported in chains to distant lands where they were made to prove how fertile they were.

MIRROR MIRROR ON THE WALL

RESEARCH IS LIKE A MAGICAL MIRROR THAT can tell you who is the fairest of them all. The taste of the jollof is in the eating, but can one eat from every plate of Jollof in Naija in search of answers? Before I put the cart before the horse, the question is this: "What is the sweetest, fairest, most delicious jollof rice in Naija and in what party ecosystem does it exist?"

Jollof rice has been known to raise its beautiful head at birthday parties, funerals, refreshment segments of meetings, naming ceremonies, wedding receptions, bukas, university campus cafeterias, secondary school dining halls, restaurants, and in the domestic settings.

Charity begins at home after all, and that dinner for two of jollof rice eaten under the influence of romantic music in the shadows afforded by dim lights is really cosy until someone farts and destroys the ambience, but yes, the rice tasted divine before the fart. Home is where mother lovingly serves the family with jollof rice that she expects all to finish. That *mama factor* is hard to resist. The domestic setting is great for impromptu cooking.

The perception of how delicious a meal is can be influenced by various factors, chief among which is hunger. The length of hunger and the intensity of the pangs produced in the stomach are directly proportional to the degree of pleasure and satisfaction derived from the murder of hunger with jollof. There is no magic mirror to ask in Naija about the best jollof, so a qualitative analysis is the only option. I would like to explain a few things about how jollof came into Naija and how the magic mirror went into the world from Africa before I introduce the research findings.

The Legend of the magic mirror

Long ago in the Songhai Empire in present day West Africa lived a great chef called Aminatu. She was famed for her delicious boiled white rice. It was as white as the insides of a coconut and her nickname, Coconut White, spread throughout the kingdom. She loved to experiment, and she developed an upgrade called jollof rice. It caused many men to lose their heads at the sight of the bright red rice she made. She was inundated with marriage proposals. The emperor's daughter, a beautiful princess called Bad Market possessed a magic mirror that could speak. It was called Ciridi, and it never lied. The Emperor's daughter was also a great cook, and she asked Ciridi who the greatest cook in Songhai was.

"Aminatu," replied the mirror. Princess Bad Market got angry and had people poison Aminatu with an apple brought in by some European travellers. Aminatu went into a trance and did not move. Her close friends, the seven short men of Songhai, built a glass casket in which she laid like a long delicious boli (roast plantain) in a Pyrex dish. Thousands of people came to look at her. One day, a prince from Nigeria came by and could not resist giving her a kiss. He had onions in his breath from his suya meal, and this made Aminatu sneeze violently and dislodge the piece of poisoned apple from her throat.

She fell in love with the Nigerian prince, moved back home with him and married him at his magnificent castle. She blessed Nigeria with her cooking skills and made Nigeria the jollof rice capital of the world.

It didn't end well for Princess Bad Market. Songhai was raided by European travellers who took her into slavery. Her magic mirror was stolen and studied. The technology was used to make smart phones, tablets and laptops, and Princess Bad Market had no reward for her invention.

In today's world, we ask a new kind of mirror the answers to pertinent questions. Data speaks, and we listen. Anything about jollof always trends on social media, but a qualitative analysis was needed to get Nigerians to explain which social settings are best for Jollof consumption.

The Food and Hygiene Department of The King Jaja of Opobo University, Opobo, conducted the study via questionnaires distributed to a random selection of Nigerians who had recently attended events and celebrations where jollof rice was served. Five main questions were asked, famously called the Opobo questions.

1.   While eating the jollof rice, did you forget all your struggles in life?

2.   At the end of the meal, did you want more?

3.   If you were invited to a similar gathering again such as a funeral, would you be more joyful at the chance of another plate of jollof rather than feel sympathy for the bereaved?

E.g. "My guy, my Papa don die."

"But your mama die last year na. Sorry" (but in your mind — hope it is the same caterer).

Or "I am getting married."

"Ha! I thought you were already."

"I divorced two years ago. I have met someone new. I would like to invite you."

"Is there going to be a reception?"

"Yes na! Even bigger than the first one. My fiancé is rich."

"No vex, na the same caterer?"

"Yes o, my mum's friend."

"I never liked that your ex-husband. But that your wedding reception jollof was to die for."

4.   Where was the setting of this jollof rice? E.g. wedding, housewarming or new job celebration.

5.   If given the chance, would you have carted plastic containers of jollof rice home?

Results

Surprisingly, the survey of over ten thousand Nigerians proved that funeral jollof rice was the most delicious. The reasons might be due to our I-cannot-kee-myself or I-cannot-koman-die mentality. After crying for the bereaved, the mourner works up an appetite and at the same time takes joy in the realisation that *where there is life, there is hope*. After the long funeral service, hunger knocks on the door in a menacing way. Many funerals take place in tribal homesteads far from the cities and fast food chains. People think of the long drive back home and eat up. Some respondents said they never stopped when driving back home for *security reasons*. The food tastes nice and is eaten in the loving memory of the deceased. At the other end of the spectrum, housewarming jollof rice scored the lowest and just above it was jollof rice at office promotion celebratory parties. Respondents scored these jollof so low one cannot but assume bias might be at play for jealous tongues don't taste accurately. In funerals, the guests are glad to be guest mourners and not the family of the bereaved, so the ability to taste is unhindered.

GLOSSARY OF NIGERIAN PIDGIN WORDS USED

Afang: Efik soup made from Afang leaves, beef, dried fish, crayfish, palm oil, and periwinkle.
Agbalagba: Yoruba word for elderly person.
Akara: Bean cake made from fried ground black-eyed beans.
Amala: Dough like meal made from yam flour and hot water. Usually served with Ewedu soup.

Banga: Palm tree fruit.

Banga soup: Soup made from Palm tree fruit.
Bukka: Roadside restaurant.Also - MamaPut and Food is ready.

Chop: 1. Food 2. Income 3. Bribe 4. Embezzle money e.g Dat Oga *chop* belle-full bifor e retire.
Choppings: Variety of food set on the table
Come chop: Small party
Congo-meat: Cooked snail
Dodo: Fried plantain

Drink garri: 1.In trouble e.g. you go *drink garri* today.2. Meal of garri and water. See Soak garri.

Eba: Meal made with garri and hot water. Usually eaten with soup with bare fingers of right hand
Fufu (Foo foo): Dough like meal made from hot water and either cassava or plantain flour. Usually served with soup

Garri: Dried cassava flour.Gen

Jollof: Paella like dish of rice made with tomatoes, peppers and spices. A Nigerian party dish.

Mama-put: Road side food seller so called because customers frequently beg for extra helpings by saying '*Mama* abeg *put* more now'.

Naija: 1. Pertaining to Nigeria 2. Nigerian citizen e.g. *Naija* no go change.
Naijaz: Plural of Naija

Oozaaroom: The private bed chamber of a couple (the other room)
Ogbono: Soup made from ground Ogbono seed of the African Mango tree, crayfish, beef, dried fish, okra, spinach and pepper.

Ogi: Pap made from corn. Also called Akamu.

Second bass jare: Catch phrase of Fela Anikulapo

Kuti used when he was exasperated with an unsavoury topic during a monologue on stage and wanted his band to get on with the music

Udogi award: Salary increases for civil servants recommended by the Udoji Review Commission that was set up in 1972
Ukodo: Meal of yams, spices, fish and pepper soup boiled in the same pot.